W9-AXN-237

Diving & Snorkeling

Bermuda

Lawson Wood

LONELY PLANET PUBLICATIONS
Melbourne • Oakland • London • Paris

Diving & Snorkeling Bermuda
- A Lonely Planet Pisces Book

1st Edition
August 1998

Published by
Lonely Planet Publications
192 Burwood Road, Hawthorn, Victoria 3122, Australia

Other offices
150 Linden Street, Oakland, California 94607, USA
10A Spring Place, London NW5 3BH, UK
71 bis rue du Cardinal Lemoine, 75005 Paris, France

Photographs by
Lawson Wood, GIS Bermuda & Bob Krist

Front cover photograph
Minnie Breslauer, Lawson Wood

Back cover photographs by
Lawson Wood, GIS Bermuda (parade)

ISBN 0 86442 573 2

Marine Biology Consultant: William S. Alevizon, Ph.D.

text and maps © Lonely Planet 1998
photographs © photographers as indicated 1998

Printed by H&Y Printing Ltd., Hong Kong

Contents

Introduction 9

Overview of Bermuda 11

Bermuda History 14

Bermuda Practicalities 19

Weather & Water **19**

Entry Requirements & Documents **19**

Getting There **22**

Getting Around **22**

Accommodations **23**

Food **24**

Money **24**

Time **25**

Banks **25**

Medical Facilities **25**

Electricity **26**

Weights & Measures **26**

Water Wear **26**

Clothing **26**

Photography **27**

Activities & Attractions 28

Fishing **28**

Golf **28**

Nature Reserves, Nature Trails & Bird Watching **28**

Sailing **29**

Helmet Diving & Glass Bottom Boats **30**

Museums & Zoos **30**

Caves **31**

Whale Watching **31**

Bermuda Beaches 32

South Shore **32**

North Shore **33**

Diving in Bermuda 34
Learning to Dive **36**

Bermuda Shipwrecks **36**

Diving Safety 38
Bermuda Recompression Facility **38**

DAN **39**

Bermuda Dive Sites 40
Pisces Rating System for Dives & Divers **43**

1   Reef: Eastern Blue Cut (Blue Hole) **48**

2   Wreck: *Constellation* **48**

3   Wreck: *Nola (Montana)* **50**

4   Wreck: *Lartington* **52**

5   Wreck: *L'Herminie* **53**

6   Reef: Chub Heads **54**

7   Wreck: *Darlington* **55**

8   Reef: Dockyards Snorkel Park **56**

9   Wreck: *Vixen* **57**

10   Wreck: *Caesar* **58**

11   Wreck: B-29 Bomber **59**

12   Wreck: *North Carolina* **60**

13   Reef: South West Breaker **60**

14   Reef: Inbetweenies **62**

15   Wreck: *Mary Celestia (Mari Celeste)* **63**

16   Wreck: *King* **65**

17   Reef: Sandy Hole **66**

18   Reef: Hole in the Wall **67**

19   Reef: Shell Hole **67**

20   Wreck: *Minnie Breslauer* **68**

21   Reef: Hangover Hole **70**

22   Wreck: *Hermes (Fogo Brava)* **71**

23   Reef: Tarpon Hole **72**

24   Wreck: *Pollockshields* **73**

25   Reef: Cathedral **74**

26   Reef: Nassa Point **75**

27   Wreck: *Pelinaion* **75**

28 Wreck: *Zovetto (Rita Zovetta)* **76**

29 Wreck: *Taunton* **77**

30 Wreck: *Manilla (Ginger Beer Bottle)* **77**

31 Wreck: *Cristóbol Colón* **78**

32 Wreck: *Madiana* **79**

33 Reef: Grotto Bay Barges **80**

34 Reef: Devil's Hole **81**

35 Reef: Flatts Bridge **82**

36 Wreck: *Xing Da* **83**

Marine Life of Bermuda **84**
Classification and Nomenclature **84**

Overview of Bermuda Marine Life **84**

Hazardous Marine Life **98**
Stinging Creatures **98**

Sea Urchins **100**

Sharks **100**

Rays **101**

Eels **102**

Scorpionfish **102**

Diving Conservation & Awareness **104**
Marine Reserves **104**

Reef Etiquette **105**

Underwater Photography & Video **108**
Underwater Photography **108**

Underwater Video **109**

Listings **112**
Accommodations **112**

Dining **113**

Diving Services **114**

Tourist Offices **115**

Publications **116**

Shipwreck Registry **118**

Index **122**

Author

Lawson Wood

A diver since 1965, Lawson Wood lives with his wife Lesley in the Scottish Borders. He is regarded as one of the world's top underwater photojournalists and authors, with over twenty years of experience in the industry. A founding member of the Marine Conservation Society and founder of the first (and only) marine nature reserve in Scotland, he has received some of the highest distinctions in photography, including a Royal Photographic Society and British Institute of Professional Photographers Fellowship (the first awarded solely for underwater photography). Lawson Wood is the author of 12 books (including three Pisces titles), and his photographs, features and articles have appeared in many different publications worldwide.

LESLEY ORSON

From the Author

This book would have been impossible without the very generous help and support from the Bermuda Ministry of Tourism and the Bermuda Tourism Office. The people from the Ministry in both the London and Bermuda offices have been friendly, courteous and above all, enthusiastic. Special mention must go to Pippa Grive, Charles Stewart, Charles Webbe and the Hon. David Dodwell M.P., as well as CIB for their help and logistical support. Michael Dolding, Wolfgang Sterrer, Margaret Potts, Diana Baudendistel, Edward Harris, Paul Leseur, Nancy Brennan and Richard Winchell (they know how they have helped!), British Airways for their support and superb international services. Alan Marquardt, who first introduced me to Bermuda diving and has helped tremendously on this project; I value his friendship greatly. Michael Burke from Blue Water Divers; Charlie Green from Nautilus Diving Ltd; Michael Heslop from Fantasea Diving; Tony Stewart from South Side Scuba; Harry Soares of Scuba Look; Lanatana Colony Club, Greenbank Guesthouse, Longtail Cliffs, and Cambridge Beaches. KJP of Edinburgh and Fuji supplied all the film. Tamron Lenses, Sea & Sea of Paignton in Devon, England for underwater lighting. Nikon UK Ltd for the help in supply of underwater and topside cameras and lenses. The Shark Group of Amble in Northumberland, England for diving equipment. And last but not least my wife Lesley, who is not only my dive buddy, she supports me in my passion—to indulge myself in our underwater world. What better place to do it than in Bermuda (where we were married).

Photography notes

The author's photographs were taken using Nikonos 111, Nikonos 1VA, Nikonos V, Nikon F-801 and Nikon F-90. Lenses used on the amphibious Nikonos system were 35 mm; 28 mm; 20 mm; 15 mm; 12 mm (and varied extension tubes supplied by Ocean Optics in London). The lenses for the housed Nikons were 14 mm; 55 mm; 85 mm; 60 mm; 105 mm; 35-70 mm zoom; Tamron supplied the 28-200 mm zoom, 20-40 mm zoom and 70-300 mm zoom lenses. Housing manufacture was by Subal in Austria and Sea & Sea in Japan.

Electronic flash was used in virtually all of the underwater photographs including the YS20; YS50; YS300 and were supplied by Sea & Sea Ltd. For the land cameras, the Nikon SB24 and SB26 were used. Additional lighting was supplied by ALS Marine Ltd from Rye in Sussex, which supplied the Nightrider Technical Lighting System; all connectors were from Camera Tech in San Francisco. Film stock used was Fujichrome Velvia; Fujichrome Provia and Fujichrome RDP. All film processing was supplied by Eastern Photocolour in Edinburgh, Scotland.

From the Publisher

This first edition was produced in Lonely Planet's U.S. office. The editor was Roslyn Bullas, with help on all fronts from Debra Miller. Hugh D'Andrade created the cover and interior design. Scott Summers handled the production and Alex Guilbert drew the maps. William Alevizon reviewed the manuscript for scientific accuracy. Portions of the Practicalities section were adapted from Lonely Planet's *Bermuda - a travel survival kit*. Special thanks to Lawson Wood for being so understanding and responsive to our seemingly unending editorial requests.

Lonely Planet Pisces Books

Lonely Planet acquired the Pisces line of diving and snorkeling books in 1997. The series will be developed and substantially revamped over the next few years, and new titles added. We invite your comments and suggestions.

Warning & Request

Even with dive guides, things change—dive site conditions, regulations, topside information. Nothing stays the same for long. Your feedback on this book will be used to help update future editions and help make the next edition more useful. Excerpts from your correspondence may appear in our newsletter, *Planet Talk*, or in the Postcards section of our website, so please let us know if you don't want your letter published or your name acknowledged.

Correspondence can be addressed to:
Lonely Planet Publications
Pisces books
150 Linden Street
Oakland, CA 94607

e-mail: info@lonelyplanet.com

BOB KRIST

Introduction

LAWSON WOOD

This guidebook describes 36 of the most popular, varied and interesting dive sites within the main Bermuda group, including the marine life of those locations. It provides enough information to help you decide whether a particular dive site is appropriate for your abilities. The dive sites covered here will give you a good sampling of the 400 or so recognized dive locations surrounding Bermuda, notwithstanding the exploratory diving being done by a few of the dive shops to the outer edges of the seamount.

Although some may consider the choice of dive sites to be rather arbitrary, this information is a reflection of my 10 years' experience diving in and around Bermuda, as well as invaluable advice from Bermuda diving operators. Each dive site description includes the site's special features and

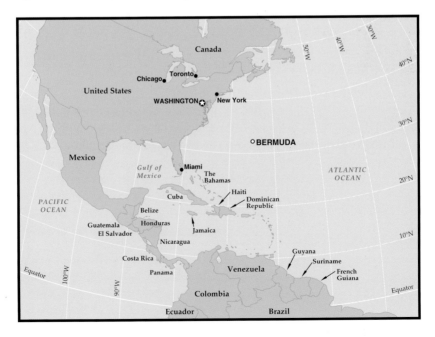

LAWSON WOOD

The tugboat *King* is easily accessible to divers and safe to explore with proper precautions.

recommended skill levels. Regardless of how you choose to read this guide—either from cover to cover or selected sections of interest—be sure to study the "Diving Safety" section before heading out.

Although the guide is aimed at active divers spending a substantial amount of time in the water, we all need to dry out sometime. The "Practicalities" and "Activities & Attractions" sections will hopefully give you a better appreciation of what else you can discover in Bermuda.

Overview of Bermuda

At the northern end of the "triangle" that bears its name, Bermuda is only 1,040 km from Cape Hatteras in the U.S. and 6,000 km from mainland Europe. This small subtropical archipelago of over 150 islands in the northern Atlantic is linked together atop a vast submarine mountain. At one time, Bermuda was a fairly substantial island, before the sea level rose with the melting of the polar caps. Created by the formation of a gigantic volcano, which rises some 4,500 meters from the seabed, the islands themselves are now the lower southeastern end of a former gigantic atoll.

Bermuda is a sprawling archipelago of over 150 islands, formed by the peaks of a massive subterranean mountain.

Bermuda is often confused with the Caribbean, which lies nearly 1,600 km south. Bermuda is not a tropical island, but a subtropical island. Situated surprisingly close to the North American coastline in the north-western Atlantic Ocean, Bermuda is on the same latitude as Dallas and is due north from San Juan in Puerto Rico. The warm waters of the Gulf Stream moderate the mild climate. The best times to visit the islands are mid April-June and October-November. The weather is warm-to-hot from April to October, which is the main tourist season and the preferred time for water activities. It is much cooler in the "winter," or low season, with a mild climate similar to spring or fall in temperate countries.

The Bermuda islands are divided into nine parishes, named after the main shareholders of the companies that sought to colonize them: St. George's, Hamilton, Smith's, Pembroke, Paget, Warwick, Devonshire, Southampton and Sandys. Bermuda's total area is about 54 sq km, shaped somewhat like a giant fish-hook, with St. George's at the top and Ireland Island in Sandys at the opposite end of the island chain. Originally descended from some sixty settlers and their slaves, Bermuda's resident population is now around 65,000. Hamilton serves as Bermuda's capital city and commercial center, offering visitors an excellent selection of restaurants, shops, an art museum and a history museum. The town of St. George, touted as Britain's second oldest settlement in the New World, is unique for its well-preserved period character, crooked streets, historic sites and museums.

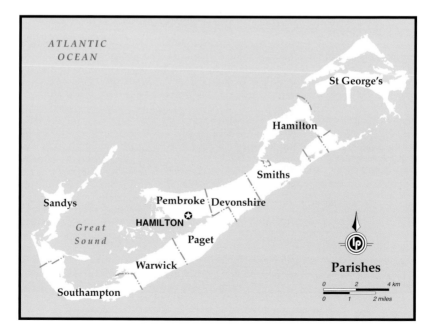

Hamilton, Bermuda's capital city, bustles with
activity and is a favorite cruise ship destination.

The main water areas around the islands are Great and Little Sounds leading into Hamilton Harbour, St. George's Harbour on the other side of the
airport and Castle Harbour at the Causeway, where several islets stop the
ocean swell coming into the sand flats. One of these is Nonsuch Island, where
William Beebe carried out some of the earliest deep water experiments in
a diving bell. Last but not least is Harrington Sound, a massive inland sea
fed only through a narrow gap at Flatts Bridge, where at slack water the shore
diving under the bridge is some of the best on the islands.

Bermudian waters—by scientific measurement—are the clearest in the
western Atlantic with 18 meter (60 ft) underwater visibility considered
poor and 54-90 meter (180-300 ft) underwater visibility the norm on the
outer reefs. Most diving in Bermuda is by boat—and the most popular way
is to go for a two-tank trip. Cost is approximately $70 and a full set of rental
equipment will cost around $50. Instruction courses are available at all lev-
els. Be prepared to show a certification card and valid log book to rent dive
equipment. If you are not certified, all the dive centers are PADI registered
and offer instruction and introductory dive lessons.

Besides diving, there are all sorts of other recreational and spectator sports
available, including fishing, hiking, birdwatching, kayaking and canoeing,
tennis, golf, whale watching, water skiing, horseback riding, caving, sailing
and glass-bottom boat cruises.

Bermuda History

LAWSON WOOD

In 1492, when Columbus "sailed the ocean blue," the trade winds probably carried him fairly close to the treacherous shores of Bermuda—he was lucky he did not end up among the other 300-400 ships that sank thereafter amid the reefs and shoals surrounding the islands. These reefs are the most northerly coral reefs in the world.

The Bermudas, or *Bermúdez,* were originally claimed for Spain by Juan de Bermúdez around 1511, but it is not known whether he set foot on *Caya de demonios*—the Isles of Devils—as they were then called. Graffiti in the form of two initials, a cross and the date 1543 carved into a rock now named Spanish Point, near Spittal Pond Nature Preserve, indicate early exploration, but these are now believed to be Portuguese in origin.

In 1609, Admiral Sir George Somers was on his way to Jamestown, Virginia, when his fleet of nine ships was scattered during a hurricane. Somers' ship, *Sea Venture,* limped along, de-masted, gradually sinking for three days before Bermuda was sighted. The crew managed to wedge *Sea Venture* between the reefs on the eastern end near the present-day Fort St. Catherine. The 150 survivors did not find any devils, but they did discover a near-paradise where the animals

This statue of Sir George Somers stands in the town of St. George.

LAWSON WOOD

14

A replication of Sir George Somers' ship, the *Sea Venture*,
which was destroyed on Bermuda's treacherous reefs.

on the islands were unafraid of man. They found giant tortoises, wild hogs, fat birds, and vast schools of fish. (The story of *Sea Venture* was the inspiration for Shakespeare's *The Tempest.*) Somers and his crew salvaged what they could of *Sea Venture*, used local wood to build two ships—*Deliverance* and *Patience*—and sailed on to Jamestown where they found pestilence, disease and famine compared to the "earthly paradise" that they had just left. In 1612, a group of 60 Englishmen became the first permanent inhabitants of Bermuda.

During the 17th century, Bermuda's economy was based on whaling, tobacco, piracy and wrecking. This was a lawless time and it was not until the end of the century that the British Crown officially took over the administration of the islands, installing a governor and an elected council of officials. As trade increased between Bermuda and America—Bermuda was very poorly supplied from Great Britain—their ties grew stronger. When America started its war of independence, George Washington looked to the islanders for help. Suffering from hunger and a surfeit of gunpowder, several Bermudians broke into Fort William and stole over 100 barrels of gunpowder, which were transported from Tobacco Bay to General Washington by fast ship. These men were never apprehended and a grateful American Congress voted to lift sanctions and provide Bermuda with a year's provisions in return for its help.

Soon Bermuda was becoming so dependent on American grain that Britain feared Bermudian allegiance to the Americans, and subsequently increased supplies and support to the islands. So much so, in fact, that America launched an attack on Bermuda in 1779 with four warships, but a British force arrived on the same day and the Americans withdrew. After thus ensuring Bermudian allegiance to the Crown, the British used Bermuda as a base from which to launch its attack on Washington D.C. in the War of 1812. The town of St. George served as the islands' capital until 1815, when the seat of government and economic power was shifted to Hamilton in the center of the island, which, incidentally, had the most ships.

On April 19, 1861, when President Lincoln announced a blockade of the Confederate ports from South Carolina to Texas, Bermudians saw this as a huge commercial opportunity, similar to those early days of piracy in the 16th century. Now with ships powered by coal and steam, they ran the Union blockades from Bermuda to several ports on the southeast coast of the United States to collect cotton for the mills in Britain in return for guns and ammunition. Wages were paid in gold and there were never problems obtaining crew, even when some of these ships came to grief amid the treacherous Bermuda reefs.

LAWSON WOOD

This land on Bermuda's eastern shores is home to present-day Fort St. Catherine and was a thankful site for the crew of the *Sea Venture,* whose sinking ship finally wrecked on the offshore reefs, close enough for the crew to make it ashore.

After the Civil War, the islands remained relatively quiet, changing their crops from tobacco to cotton. Bermuda was also becoming world famous for her onions. Discovered in 1845 by a sea captain, John D. Bell of Southampton in the Canary Islands, the small white onion, with an especially sweet and mild taste, thrived in Bermuda's climate. It eventually became Bermuda's greatest export, but in time was superseded by cheaper marketing and vastly greater output from American farmers (who even called one of the main onion-growing areas in Texas "Bermuda"!).

Many Bermudians volunteered for active service during WWI, and two separate battalions of black and white soldiers served in France, as well as in defense of the islands, earning distinctions. During prohibition, Bermuda was once more inexorably linked with the U.S., like so many offshore islands in the Caribbean. The Volstaed Act was instrumental in bringing the first tourists to the islands, not in search of paradise, but in search of whiskey. This massive influx of people and money into the islands changed Bermudian life forever.

During WWII, Bermuda was the center for the "trappers," men and women recruited from England to intercept messages between the U.S. and

Nazi Germany. Operating from the cellars of the Princess Hotel, about 1,200 men and women were taught to decipher microdot messages to trap German spies operating in the U.S.

After the war, American and Canadian companies began investing heavily in Bermuda because of the low taxation. In the 1970s, the number of so-called exempt companies registered in Bermuda doubled, bringing an unprecedented source of income to an otherwise failing economy.

In the 1980s, the issue of independence from Britain became a dominant political theme, and in 1995 a referendum was held. But, despite the years of debate the independence issue had evoked, just 25% of the electorate voted in favor of breaking ties with Britain. In the end many Bermudians, regardless of their political affiliations, were apprehensive about the potential political and economic cost of independence.

Bermuda Practicalities

BOB KRIST

Weather & Water

Bermuda enjoys a mild, agreeable climate. The average annual high temperature is 24°C (75°F), while the average annual low temperature is 20°C (68°F). In the warmest months, July to September, the average high temperature is 30°C (85°F) and the average low is 24°C (75°F). The coldest months, January to March, have an average high temperature of 21°C (69°F) and an average low of 15°C (60°F).

Relative humidity is high all year round, ranging from an average of 75% in March to 84% in August. The mean annual rainfall is 145 cm (57 inches), distributed fairly evenly over the year with no real rainy season.

While Bermuda is not in the main hurricane belt that whips across the Caribbean, it does occasionally get nipped by such storms if they blow back out to sea in a northerly direction.

The water temperature from November to April averages about 18-22°C (65-71°F). Underwater visibility is at its best then, and ranges from 30-60 meters (100-200 ft). From May to October the water temperature is warmer, from 24-30°C (75-86°F). During this time visibility is in the 24-30 meter (80-100 ft) range. The warmest month is August, when visibility is at its lowest, around 18-24 meters (60-80 ft).

Entry Requirements & Documents

A passport is the preferred document for entry into Bermuda and is required of visitors from all countries that require a passport for re-entry. Visas are not required for visitors from the U.K., U.S., Canada, Western Europe, Australia and New Zealand. All visitors landing in Bermuda must be in possession of a return or onward ticket. Immigration authorities will determine your permitted length of stay. They commonly grant a stay of up to 21 days, which can be renewed. No vaccinations are required. Certified divers should bring their C-cards and log books.

ATLANTIC
OCEAN

**_Constellation_ and
Nola wrecks**

Two of the most popular shipwreck
dives, and inspiration for the book
and movie _The Deep_

Dockyards Snorkel Park

Excellent for shallow snorkeling
and for exploring inshore reefs

Ireland
Island
North

Ireland
Island
South

Spanish
Point

_Long
Bay_

Boaz
Island

Somerset
Island

_Great
Sound_

_Little
Sound_

The South Western
Area

South Shore Park

This coastal park contains many
of Bermuda's finest beaches

Southwest Breaker

Spectacular dive site with
extensive underwater tunnel
and cavern system running
completely under the reef

**_Hermes_ and
Minnie Breslauer wrecks**

Popular South Shore dives, only
minutes from local dive shops

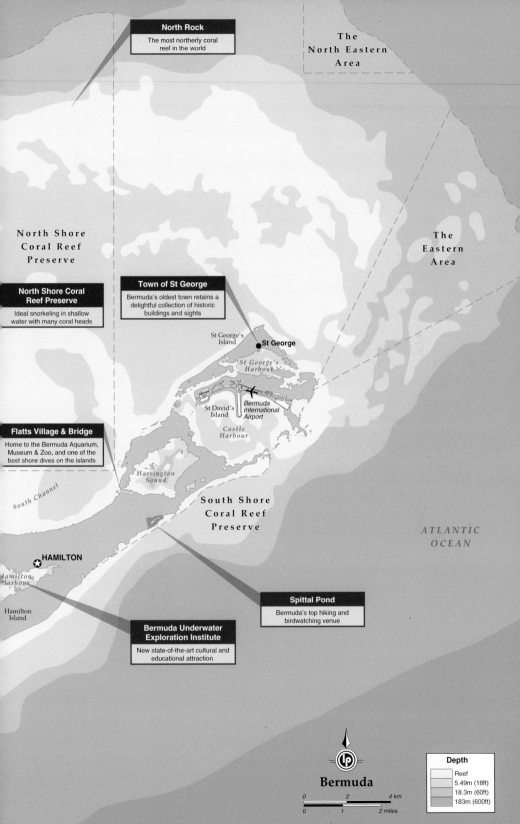

North Rock

The most northerly coral reef in the world

The
North Eastern
Area

North Shore
Coral Reef
Preserve

**North Shore Coral
Reef Preserve**

Ideal snorkeling in shallow
water with many coral heads

Town of St George

Bermuda's oldest town retains a
delightful collection of historic
buildings and sights

The
Eastern
Area

St George's
Island

● St George

St George's
Harbour

Flatts Village & Bridge

Home to the Bermuda Aquarium,
Museum & Zoo, and one of the
best shore dives on the islands

St David's
Island

Bermuda
International
Airport

Castle
Harbour

Harrington
Sound

South Channel

South Shore
Coral Reef
Preserve

ATLANTIC
OCEAN

✪ **HAMILTON**

Hamilton
Harbour

Spittal Pond

Bermuda's top hiking and
birdwatching venue

Hamilton
Island

**Bermuda Underwater
Exploration Institute**

New state-of-the-art cultural and
educational attraction

LP

Bermuda

0   2   4 km

0   1   2 miles

not for navigation

Depth	
	Reef
	5.49m (18ft)
	18.3m (60ft)
	183m (600ft)

GIS BERMUDA

St. George, one of the oldest English settlements in the New World,
is quiet and quaint with many fine restaurants and heritage centers.

Getting There

There are regular flights to Bermuda each week from London and Frank-
furt, and daily flights from New York, Newark, Atlanta, Baltimore, Charlotte
and Boston, as well as cities in Canada.

Arriving by air (try to get a window seat) will give you a panoramic view
of some 150 islands and inlets dotting the emerald, sapphire and turquoise
colors of the sea as it changes according to depth, reflecting the sunlight from
the pink and white sand.

Security at the airport is the same as at American destinations. As long
as you have a valid return air ticket and proof of where you are staying, there
should be little delay. There is a $20 departure tax payable at the airport.

Getting Around

Transportation is by ferry, bus, taxi, scooter, moped and bicycle. *There are
no rental cars.* The government operates the bus and ferry services. By far
the most popular way of getting around the islands is by scooter, which costs
about $25 per day. Driving is on the left, and deference is always given to

the pedestrian. The speed limit throughout Bermuda is 35 km per hour, except in the main towns, such as St. George and Hamilton, where it drops to 25 km per hour. Your tour operator can arrange your transportation before you leave home, but I suggest that you arrange everything after you arrive on the island because it will cost less and you will be able to inspect the scooter of your choice.

Public buses and private minibuses are another alternative to getting around the islands and are very cheap compared to taxis. Small dories are another option and can be chartered from marinas, allowing you to visit the outer islands at your leisure. Glass-bottomed boats, of course, will allow you to see the reefs without getting your feet wet. Ferries operate regularly between Hamilton and the Dockyard, linking a few of the nearby islands. There is also a helicopter service, which operates from St. David's and takes four passengers on island sightseeing tours.

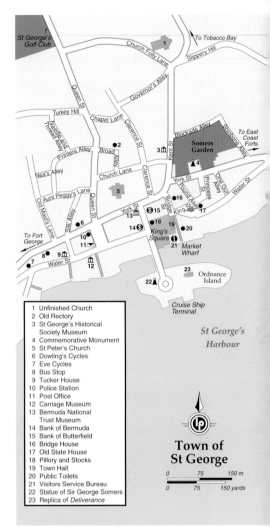

1 Unfinished Church
2 Old Rectory
3 St George's Historical
   Society Museum
4 Commemorative Monument
5 St Peter's Church
6 Dowling's Cycles
7 Eve Cycles
8 Bus Stop
9 Tucker House
10 Police Station
11 Post Office
12 Carriage Museum
13 Bermuda National
   Trust Museum
14 Bank of Bermuda
15 Bank of Butterfield
16 Bridge House
17 Old State House
18 Pillory and Stocks
19 Town Hall
20 Public Toilets
21 Visitors Service Bureau
22 Statue of Sir George Somers
23 Replica of *Deliverance*

St George's Harbour

Town of St George

0   75   150 m
0   75   150 yards

Accommodations

Bermuda has no truly budget accommodations—no youth hostels, YMCAs, family campgrounds, or economy-chain motels. As a general rule, the most economical options are tourist apartments, which come completely furnished. Other accommodations options include upmarket "cottages," small guest houses with limited services, and resort hotels with all the usual resort facilities, including swimming pools, room service, sports facilities and restaurants. You can also house-sit for Bermudians who spend time overseas, and an advertisement placed in the local newspaper may be all it takes to either swap your own home, or to house-sit.

Food

Food, like everything else, tends to be expensive in Bermuda. On the plus side, Bermuda offers a good variety of dining options, from side-street delis to superb fine-dining restaurants. While the upmarket restaurants commonly focus on French-inspired fare, moderately priced eateries cover a wide gamut. At the low end there are pizzerias, sandwich shops and fast-food outlets. A service charge of around 15% is added to most meals in the better restaurants.

Money

The currency unit is the Bermuda dollar (BD$), which is pegged at a 1:1 ratio with the U.S. dollar. It's most convenient to carry U.S. currency, as both U.S. dollars and traveler's checks are accepted by most businesses. Change is usually given in local currency. Exchange rates are standard throughout the islands in both shops and banks. Major credit cards, such as Visa, MasterCard and American Express, are accepted by most shops (including dive centers) and restaurants. Hotels and guesthouses are more fickle on credit cards, however. Ask whether credit cards are honored before you book accommodations.

The Bermuda Day parade is a celebration of Bermuda's colorful past.

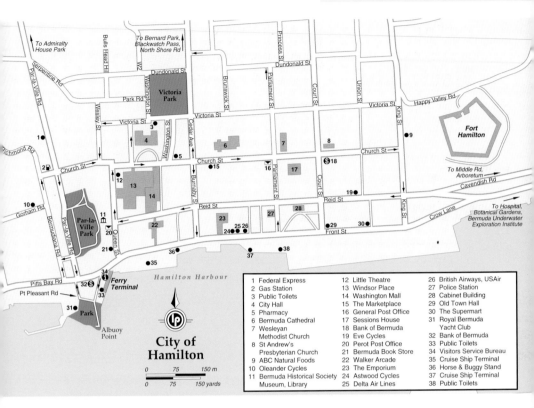

City of
Hamilton

1 Federal Express	12 Little Theatre	26 British Airways, USAir
2 Gas Station	13 Windsor Place	27 Police Station
3 Public Toilets	14 Washington Mall	28 Cabinet Building
4 City Hall	15 The Marketplace	29 Old Town Hall
5 Pharmacy	16 General Post Office	30 The Supermart
6 Bermuda Cathedral	17 Sessions House	31 Royal Bermuda
7 Wesleyan	18 Bank of Bermuda	Yacht Club
Methodist Church	19 Eve Cycles	32 Bank of Bermuda
8 St Andrew's	20 Perot Post Office	33 Public Toilets
Presbyterian Church	21 Bermuda Book Store	34 Visitors Service Bureau
9 ABC Natural Foods	22 Walker Arcade	35 Cruise Ship Terminal
10 Oleander Cycles	23 The Emporium	36 Horse & Buggy Stand
11 Bermuda Historical Society	24 Astwood Cycles	37 Cruise Ship Terminal
Museum, Library	25 Delta Air Lines	38 Public Toilets

Time

Bermuda is in the Atlantic Standard Time zone, which is 4 hours behind GMT and 1 hour ahead of Eastern Standard Time.

Banks

The Bank of Bermuda, Bank of Butterfield and Bermuda Commercial Bank will exchange foreign currency and traveler's checks. Banks at the airport are always open for arrivals and departures of international flights. Most of the international hotels will also exchange your currency at the same rate as the banks.

Medical Facilities

King Edward VII Memorial Hospital is the only hospital on Bermuda. It is located on Point Finger Rd., Paget ☎ 441-236-2345. It has a full 24-hour emergency room. Visitors requiring treatment must pay in advance of a hospital stay or after treatment. Be sure to keep all of your receipts for subsequent insurance claims. The nearest full hyperbaric recompression facilities are also located at the hospital.

Electricity

Electric current operates on 110 volts and 60 cycles, and the U.S.-style flat, two-pronged plug is used. Some hotels have adapters for electric shavers. If you require 220 volts for recharging camera lamps or strobes, you may find it better to bring an adapter with you or ask the diving operation you are using for assistance.

Weights & Measures

Although the conversion to metric was implemented in such areas as the posting of speed limits, Bermuda still uses the imperial system of measurement for many applications. Newspapers print temperatures in degrees Fahrenheit and most weights are measured in ounces and pounds.

Water Wear

When diving and snorkeling it's best to wear a Lycra skin in summer or a wetsuit in winter. These will protect you against coral abrasions and stings from planktonic creatures in the water, as well as the fierce sun on the surface. Although Bermuda lies within range of the warm Gulf Stream sweeping up from the Caribbean, the water does get chilly during the winter and spring months and you will get cold in anything less than a full 7 mm (½-inch) wetsuit. Some divers now use dry suits during the winter when the water temperatures drop.

Clothing

Women wear light cotton dresses, slacks and shorts at any time of the year. Formal dress is seldom worn in the evening, but can be required in a few of the more upscale hotels and restaurants. Topless sunbathing is not allowed on any of the beaches and discretion should be observed when among locals. For men, lightweight slacks or shorts and open neck shirts are a

Bermuda Shorts

Bermuda shorts are the closest thing Bermuda has to a national dress for men. They were originally inspired by British troops stationed in hot climates overseas, when the soldiers would trim the lower legs of their uniforms to make them more bearable in the heat. By the 1920s, Bermuda men had adopted such shorts as the standard wear for all smart and casual dressing, wearing them in the office, or on the golf course.

good choice. When visiting the main towns or entering restaurants, shops, banks and post offices, swim wear should *not* be worn, and shirts, shorts and shoes are mandatory. While "smart casual" wear will get you a table at most restaurants, there are still a number of top-end restaurants that require jackets and ties, so it's always wise to inquire about dress codes when making a dinner reservation. Pack a windbreaker and perhaps jeans and a sweatshirt for riding the scooters at night. Blustery squalls also hit the islands and portable rainwear should also be packed.

Photography

There are several film processing locations in Bermuda, most of which are of the same-day variety. Only a few facilities can handle E-6 slide processing on site. Bermuda Photo Craftsmen, Walker Arcade, Hamilton ☎ 441-295-2698; Kodak Express (3 locations), Washington Mall, Hamilton ☎ 441-295-2519; Quality Color, 3 Park Rd., Hamilton ☎ 441-292-8100; Stuart's, P.O. Box HM 2705, Hamilton ☎ 441-295-5496.

Refer to the "Underwater Photography & Video" section later in this book for advice on equipment and technique. Some underwater photographic equipment can be rented from dive centers.

LAWSON WOOD

Activities & Attractions

BOB KRIST

Fishing

Bermuda is world renowned for its deep-sea fishing, and many charter boats travel to the outer reefs and drop off to catch marlin, kingfish, sailfish and tuna. The best conditions are from May to November. Sport fishers are encouraged to release game fish, particularly marlin and other billfish, unless they're being taken for food.

Golf

There are currently eight golf courses on Bermuda, all of international standard and most with breathtaking coastal scenery. Six are open to the public (Belmont Gold Club, Castle Harbour Golf Club, Ocean View Golf Course, Port Royal Golf Course, Southampton Princess Golf Club and St. George's Golf Club) and two require introduction by members (Mid Ocean Club and Riddell's Bay Golf & Country Club).

Nature Reserves, Nature Trails & Bird Watching

There are several nature reserves in Bermuda that serve as a good introduction to Bermuda flora and fauna. Birders and naturalists will find a wealth of life amid the islands' numerous nature trails and preserves set in Bermuda's parishes and islands. The largest and most accessible reserve is **Spittal Pond** in Smith's Parish, where you can see wild flamingo, herons and egrets, toads and tree frogs. The **Botanical Gardens**, just north of Hamilton, are well worth a visit, with excellent

LAWSON WOOD

The national bird of Bermuda is the Bermuda longtail.

Spanish moss covers many ancient Bermuda cedar trees.

exhibits and a kiosk detailing the different flora and fauna. Other areas include: **The Arboretum** along Middle Rd., Devonshire; **Penhurst Park** on Middle Rd., Smith's; **Admiralty Park** at Spanish Point in Pembroke, which has walking trails, sea caves, swimming and picnic grounds; **Ely's Harbour** in Sandys Parish, which has trails, a picnic area, swimming, and a chapel dating back to 1616; and the **Bermuda Railway Trail,** which winds from end to end of the island and includes the former railway track.

The best months for bird watching are from November to April when the islands receive many interesting migratory visitors. Tours are organized regularly by the Bermuda Audubon Society and the Parks Ranger and Government Conservation Officer.

Sailing

Bermuda has no shortage of sailing locales, with the greatest abundance found in the protected waters of the Great Sound and Little Sound. Small skiffs can be rented from most marinas. During May, June, July, August and October, the Royal Bermuda Yacht Club sponsors a variety of international races, attracting sailors and yachts from all over the world.

Helmet Diving & Glass Bottom Boats

Helmet diving offers visitors a chance to jump beneath the surface of the water without having to master diving skills. The diving helmet works like a glass turned upside down in water, with fresh air supplied by a hose. Excess bubbles escape naturally from the underside. The "dive," which lasts about 30 minutes, occurs at the sandy edge of the reef in about 3 meters of water, allowing fish and coral to be viewed up close. Greg Hartley runs this operation from his boat the *Rainbow Runner* ☎ 441-234-2861.

There are a number of excellent glass bottom boat operators with many years of experience in Bermuda waters. Most will combine a snorkel tour and you will be able to explore the shipwrecks *Vixen*, *Constellation* and *Nola*.

Museums & Zoos

The Bermuda Underwater Exploration Institute This new attraction in Hamilton houses several important collections of marine exhibits detailing aspects of marine archaeology that have led to some of the most exciting finds in maritime history. Oriented around interactive education and using a multimedia presentation facility, this is a superb addition to the islands' eco-tourism theme. One of the highlights is "The Dive," a simulated journey to the ocean depths ☎ 441-292-7219; fax 441-236-6141.

The Bermuda Maritime Museum The maritime museum is situated on Ireland Island in Sandys Parish and adjacent to the old Naval Dockyard. The museum contains exhibits on Bermuda's maritime heritage, and includes relics from the *Sea Venture*, ancient maps, naval artifacts and treasures recovered from Spanish wrecks by Teddy Tucker, Bermuda's famed treasure diver ☎ 441-234-1333; fax 441-234-1735.

The Bermuda Maritime Museum at the old Naval Dockyard has detailed exhibits of Bermuda's nautical heritage.

The Bermuda Biological Station for Research The station conducts research from the special perspective of a mid-ocean island to educate future scientists and to provide well equipped facilities and technical staff to support visiting scientists, faculty and students from all over the world. The station is open for guided tours each Wednesday morning ☎ 441-297-1880; fax 441-297-8143.

Flatts Bridge Aquarium, Museum & Zoo The new North Rock exhibit is a celebration of Bermuda's marine life heritage. The exhibit shows the reefs and marine creatures found around Bermuda's North Rock, the world's most northerly coral reef. The zoo has also been instrumental in the re-introduction of the endangered Caribbean flamingo into the British Virgin Islands on the island of Anegada ☎ 441-293-2727; fax 441-293-8944.

Caves

There are two sets of caves accessible to the public. **Crystal Caves** and **Leamington's Amber Caves** have vast underground chambers filled with pristine stalagmites, stalactites, flow stone and other natural limestone creations. Scuba divers can access some of the chambers from the ocean and Harrington Sound. Guided tours are offered daily in each set of caves. Crystal Caves, Wilkinson Avenue off Harrington Sound Rd., Bailey's Bay, Hamilton Parish ☎ 441-293-0640. Leamington's Amber Caves, Harrington Sound Rd., Hamilton Parish ☎ 441-293-1188.

Whale Watching

Whale watching trips are becoming increasingly popular in Bermuda. Humpback whales, migrating from the Silver Banks in the eastern Caribbean north to Nova Scotia, are sometimes seen as they pass by the islands in April and May. Although there are no regularly scheduled trips, dive boats from most of the dive centers often take non-divers out to areas where whales have been spotted during whale season, conditions and demand permitting.

Bermuda Beaches

Bermuda has some of the best beaches in the world. All are very popular and many have the associated watersports (and noise); others are calm, secluded and quiet. The best are located along the south shore from Tucker's Town to Southampton. Only a few hotels are actually located on the ocean front, but because the island is so small, the beaches can be reached by foot or scooter, motorbike or taxi. The South Shore beaches are protected by coral reefs that break the swell. Most are shallow and offer superb snorkeling. In contrast, the best beaches along North Shore offer deeper water for snorkeling, and rock pools to explore amid secluded sheltered coves.

South Shore

Elbow Beach in Paget is popular with both tourists and locals; non-residents can pay $5 to use the hotel's facilities.

Horseshoe Bay in Warwick is probably the most popular and populated beach in Bermuda and has a spectacular crescent-shaped beach with all the necessary facilities.

Warwick Long Bay in Warwick is a long white stretch of sand with a steep beach and rolling surf. It stretches from Longtail Cliffs all the way to Jobson's Cove.

Jobson's Cove, Stonehole Bay and **Chaplin Bay** in Warwick have majestic rock formations and all are very secluded.

John Smith's Bay in Smith's is named after Capt. John Smith, a 17th century adventurer. The beach has moderate surf and conveniences.

Devonshire Bay in Devonshire is calm, sheltered and nearly hidden from sight. Perfect for children. The beach has fascinating pools and local fishermen sell their catches here.

Clearwater Beach Recreation and Nature Area in St. David's is extremely popular. Nature trails, beautiful beaches, playgrounds and facilities.

Astwood Beach and Park has steep cliffs and picnic tables with snorkeling in a sheltered sandy cove and the usual conveniences.

Church Bay in Southampton is a tiny and beautiful beach with an ancient fort; ideal for snorkeling; public conveniences.

West Whale Bay in Sandys is a very pink beach lying beneath a ruined fort on a hill. There is excellent snorkeling in this bay that was once used by whalers. Whales are seen regularly offshore during the spring, and whale-watching boat trips can be arranged.

Mangrove Bay in Sandys is protected with calm, shallow water that is ideal for children and non-swimmers.

Maritime Museum Snorkel Trail in Sandys extends to the west of the ancient Maritime Fort. The well laid out trail is marked by cannons from the 16th and 17th centuries. You can see soft and hard corals and lots of fish all located in a well protected area next to the fort's walls ☎ 441-292-8652; fax 441-292-5193.

North Shore

Tobacco Bay in St. George has some spectacular ancient coral formations and is superb for snorkeling. Snack bar and changing facilities.

Shelly Bay in Hamilton Parish is a shell-covered beach also named after one of the islands' original colonists. The water is shallow and filled with fish, ideal for snorkeling.

Admiralty House in Pembroke has a calm swimming area known as Clarence Cove. There are walking routes, cliffs and sea caves to explore.

Many of the beaches along the south shore are sheltered and secluded.

Diving in Bermuda

LAWSON WOOD

Whether you want to try scuba diving for the first time, earn an international diving certificate, or just expand your diving horizons, Bermuda is an excellent diving destination. Bermuda is the only location in the world where sport divers can dive on a vast number of shipwrecks spanning 500 years of nautical history; in fact, Bermuda tops diving polls as having the best wreck diving in the world.

Most of Bermuda's dive sites are a 10-40-minute boat ride from the shore opposite the dive centers, some of which offer free transportation to and from your hotel. The first dive of the day is usually to a wreck in generally 20-24 meters (65-80 ft), with running times to the dive sites rarely more than 40 minutes, even to the farthest reefs and wrecks. Then there is a 1½ hour break before your second dive on a shallow reef at 8-18 meters (25-60 ft). Fantasea Diving & Snorkeling and Blue Water Divers cover the most area and are not averse to traveling for over an hour to some of the farther offshore reefs and wrecks, weather permitting.

There are several new wrecks situated close to the major diving centers. These wrecks have been deliberately sunk in prime sites to attract more fish and add interest to reef dives, and are all rewarding and photogenic dives. They are well encrusted in marine life, except for the *Xing Da* sunk in 1997. One of the most popular sites is the *Hermes,* sunk in 1984 off Warwick Bay. Mooring buoys have been placed at all of the prime sites to avoid damaging the reef.

The reefs and surrounding continental shelf have been fished commercially for many years with indiscriminate fish traps, almost denuding the reef in some areas. With a new conservation awareness, fish traps have been completely banned, and the collecting of corals and shells is prohibited, though dead or empty shells may be collected in specific areas. Spear guns are banned. Spear fishing is not allowed within one mile of shore and no more than two fish of a single species may be speared within a 24-hour period.

LAWSON WOOD

The mast of the *Hermes*, which was deliberately sunk in 1984 as an artificial reef, is very popular with visiting divers.

Learning to Dive

Bermuda is an excellent place to get your diving certification. In addition to the full certification courses offered by all of Bermuda's dive operators, most operations offer resort courses and instruction. A resort course will provide you with a half-day orientation in the classroom, swimming pool practice, and an open ocean dive onto a shallow reef or wreck. Resort courses are not certification courses, but are a good way to experience diving quickly, perhaps before taking a full-fledged certification course.

Bermuda Shipwrecks

What was once a navigator's nightmare is now a wreck diver's dream come true. Bermuda is the only location in the world where divers can come into contact with such a range of shipwrecks. Virtually all of the ships went down on shallow reefs, allowing maximum bottom time for exploration. Much research has been carried out around the islands, principally by Teddy Tucker, a descendent of one of the first colonizing families of Bermuda. Tucker has charted, recorded and salvaged many vessels, some of which have yielded incredible wealth, not only in treasure, but also in information.

While modern salvage techniques are increasingly sophisticated, they're no substitute for hard work and perseverance. The problem, when searching for a recorded wreck site, is that in all probability the actual wreck may be nowhere near the pile of ballast stones (carried in the hull of ships for

A cannon from the wreck of *L'Herminie* rests on the seabed and makes a great photographic subject.

LAWSON WOOD

Archival Research

The lure of so many shipwrecks and the chance for discovering treasure has resulted in a wealth of written legacy concerning these quests. Much of this information is available to researchers at the following places:

Bermuda Archives, 30 Parliament St., Hamilton ☎ 441-295-5151.
Bermuda Underwater Exploration Institute, 40 Crow Lane, Hamilton
  ☎ 441-292-7219.
Bermuda Library, Queen St., Hamilton ☎ 441-295-2905.
Bermuda Historical Society Museum, 13 Queen St., Hamilton
  ☎ 441-295-2487.

stability) where the ship originally sank. As the wooden ships were driven onto the reef during storms, the jagged corals would rip out the bottom of the hull and the ballast stones would be dumped, leaving the rest of the stricken ship to roll and tumble over the other coral heads at the mercy of tidal currents and weather. In many cases there were no survivors to tell the tale, and very few reference points on submerged reefs. It's likely that there are hundreds more wrecks still waiting to be discovered.

Now divers are able to explore most of Bermuda's known shipwrecks. However, *do not dive inside a shipwreck unless you have specialized training, have the proper equipment, and are under the supervision of a qualified wreck and antiquity diving expert.* It is much better and safer to explore shipwrecks from the outside.

All of Bermuda's shipwrecks are protected by law, and no unauthorized excavation, interference, or removal of any objects of marine or historical interest is allowed. If a new wreck or site of antiquity is discovered, nothing must be touched, the site position details should be accurately taken, and the appropriate authorities should be notified. Dr. Edward Harris, the director of the Bermuda Maritime Museum, welcomes new information on Bermuda shipwrecks, and can let visiting divers know how they can help in any ongoing archaeological projects around the islands ☎ 441-234-1333; Email: marmuse@ibl.com.

Diving Safety

LAWSON WOOD

Diving is a safe sport and there are very few accidents compared to the number of divers and number of dives made each year. However, there are some basic precautions you should take before leaving home.

Be sure that any personal diving equipment is properly serviced and in good working order. Regulators in particular are prone to malfunction. Carry an extra mask, especially if you have prescription lenses, and check that all of your fin straps, buckles and BC straps are not corroded or worn. If you have done little recent diving, enroll in a refresher course at home or in Bermuda to reacquaint yourself with open water techniques, especially before diving in some of the deeper sites. The dive centers in Bermuda have late-model, regularly serviced rental equipment. This is a good option if you don't own your own, or don't wish to bring your gear with you, particularly when traveling long distances. Renting equipment that you can rely on is well worth any financial considerations.

Whatever equipment you use, you should assess each dive prior to entering the water and, if unsure of the dive details, get firsthand knowledge from a local dive guide or instructor. Dive conditions do vary, even during a dive, and divers should be aware of what to do in any given situation. If you have any doubt about your diving skill level or conditions of the dive, discuss your concerns with the operator you are diving with. When the infrequent injury does occur while diving, it's imperative to summon the appropriate medical personnel as quickly as possible.

Bermuda Recompression Facility

Bermuda's hyperbaric recompression facilities are located at the 324-bed King Edward VII Memorial Hospital in Paget ☎ 441-236-2345. Dial 911 to summon an ambulance.

Dive Safety Services

While the proportion of diving accidents is low, accidents do happen, and emergency treatment should be sought immediately. Bermuda diving operators are equipped to handle most medical emergencies and have ship-to-shore radio to summon extra help. The islands' recompression chamber is located in the hospital in Paget.

Recompression Chamber King Edwards Memorial Hospital, Point Finger Rd. & Berry Rd., Paget ☎ 441-236-2345.

Air and Sea Rescue ☎ 441-297-1010

Marine Police ☎ 441-295-0011

DAN (Divers Alert Network) ☎ 919-648-4326 (emergency only, 24-hours a day) Website: www.dan.ycg.org

DAN

Divers Alert Network (DAN) is an international membership association of individuals and organizations sharing a common interest in diving and safety. It operates a 24-hour diving emergency hotline, ☎ 919-684-8111 or 919-684-4DAN (919-684-4DAN (-4326) accepts collect calls in a dive emergency). DAN does not directly provide medical care; however, it does provide advice on early treatment, evacuation, and hyperbaric treatment of diving-related injuries. Divers should contact DAN for assistance as soon as a diving emergency is suspected. DAN membership is reasonably priced and includes DAN TravelAssist, a membership benefit, which covers medical air evacuation from anywhere in the world for any illness or injury. For a small additional fee, divers can get secondary insurance coverage for decompression illness. For membership questions call 800-446-2671 in the U.S. or 919-684-2948 elsewhere.

Bermuda
Dive Sites

The main group of the Bermuda islands is actually the coralline limestone tips of a submarine volcanic plateau, which have virtually formed an atoll that, over time, has been covered with dense, scrubby vegetation. Below the reach of the tide, the sea floor is divided into a number of different reef habitats. Closest to shore is the *fringing reef*. It is usually flat and sandy on the top, with the occasional knob of hard coral. Amidst the coral outcroppings patches of turtle grass are found growing in open sand areas.

Farther out, the sea floor slopes down to an outer fringing reef, or forms a much larger barrier reef consisting largely of star and brain corals topped by sea fans, sea whips and other soft corals. The sea floor then becomes more steeply inclined, and consists of open sand interspersed with low encrusting clumps of hard and soft coral, often attached to the ancient limestone skeletons of the reefs. These features are sometimes known as *bommies*, but are more generally referred to as a *patch reef* system. Some of the inner sections of reef are so large they have created mini-walls that are also covered in encrusting corals (there are no true drop-offs in Bermuda). These inshore coral reefs are interspersed with gullies, canyons, tunnels and caves.

A term almost synonymous with Bermuda is *breaker*. This is a patch of reef that rises to the sea surface. When the sea is rough, the waves break over the reef and the formation is easily spotted; but when the sea is calm, these reefs are often the cause of many a shipwreck.

Different coral species form colonies of many shapes and sizes. What you are actually seeing of the reef is only the thin, living outer layer, which grows over the ancient skeletons of past generations. Bermuda's coral reef dive sites are composed primarily of ancient coralline rock, and have been heavily encrusted over the centuries by a large variety of marine growth. At these sites you'll see many of the typical fish and invertebrate species characteristic of the tropical western Atlantic Ocean. Most diving, however, is done on the many shipwrecks that have come to grief around the islands' treacherous ring of reefs.

Some 400 shipwrecks dot the reefs, shoals and lagoons of Bermuda. This book focuses on 22 of the most popular wrecks, and an additional 14 reef sites, for a broad spectrum of diving experiences. These sites are regarded as some of the most interesting historically, photographically and zoologically.

Diving around Bermuda is seasonal, and conditions do vary. It is always advisable to check with your dive operator to find out which areas are being dived and what the prevailing water and weather conditions are at a particular time.

Bermuda is especially accommodating because the many lee shores and sheltered conditions permit top-notch diving during all seasons.

Bermuda Cave Diving

Bermuda has other challenging dives in the many caves and limestone caverns on the islands. Many of these caverns have been mapped by the Bermuda branch of the British Sub Aqua Club and members will accompany divers who have cave diving training. Other challenging dives are found offshore on the Challenger and Argos banks many miles south of Bermuda. Argos is a submarine seamount that once held a U.S. listening station for Soviet submarines. This was destroyed during a violent hurricane a number of years ago and the remains were dynamited in 1975. This very deep dive is at the limit of scuba diving exploration of the mid-western Atlantic. If you plan to do any cave diving in Bermuda, you should have specialized training and always be accompanied by someone knowledgeable and familiar with the local conditions.

Most of the diving centers are now open all year to cater to an increasing number of winter divers. The water is much cooler in the winter and the sea a little rougher, but with wetsuits or even drysuits, you can still visit all of the offshore wreck sites and enjoy some incredibly clear water.

Bermuda's oceanic isolation and the fact it is bathed in the warm waters of the Gulf Stream have accounted for many indigenous species unique to Bermuda's waters. Divers should watch for blue angelfish (*Holocanthus bermudensis*) and anemone shrimp *(Periclimenes anthophilus)*. All of the coral sea fans, although not as diverse as those found in the Caribbean, are in excellent condition, and there are some very large mature specimens. The inner reefs are a labyrinth of cavernous tunnels, caves and spectacular arches.

LAWSON WOOD

During the summer months, thousands of silversides can be found in the Western Blue Cut.

Pisces Rating System for Dives & Divers

The dive sites in this book are rated according to the following diver skill level rating system. These are not absolute ratings but apply to divers at a particular time, diving at a particular place. For instance, someone unfamiliar with prevailing conditions might be considered a novice diver at one dive area, and an intermediate diver at another, more familiar location.

Novice: A novice diver generally fits the following profile:
◆ basic scuba certification from an internationally recognized certifying agency
◆ dives infrequently (less than one trip a year)
◆ logged fewer than 25 total dives
◆ dives no deeper than 18 meters (60 ft)
◆ little or no experience diving in similar waters and conditions
* *A novice diver should be accompanied by an instructor or divemaster on all dives*

Intermediate: An intermediate diver generally fits the following profile:
◆ may have participated in some form of continuing diver education
◆ logged between 25 and 100 dives
◆ dives no deeper than 40 meters (130 ft)
◆ has been diving within the last six months in similar waters and conditions

Advanced: An advanced diver generally fits the following profile:
◆ advanced certification
◆ has been diving for more than 2 years; logged over 100 dives
◆ has been diving within the last six months in similar waters and conditions

Regardless of skill level, you should be in good physical condition and know your limitations. If you are uncertain as to which category you fit, ask the advice of a local dive instructor. He or she is best qualified to assess your abilities based on the prevailing dive conditions at any given site. Ultimately you must decide if you are capable of making a particular dive, depending on your level of training, recent experience, and physical condition, as well as water conditions at the site. Remember that water conditions can change at any time, even during a dive.

Bermuda Dive Sites

	Good Snorkeling	Novice	Intermediate	Advanced
1 Reef: Eastern Blue Cut (Blue Hole)	✓		✓	✓
2 Wreck: Constellation	✓	✓	✓	✓
3 Wreck: Nola (Montana)	✓	✓	✓	✓
4 Wreck: Lartington	✓	✓	✓	✓
5 Wreck: L'Herminie	✓	✓	✓	✓
6 Reef: Chub Heads			✓	✓
7 Wreck: Darlington		✓	✓	✓
8 Reef: Dockyards Snorkel Park	✓	✓	✓	✓
9 Wreck: Vixen	✓	✓	✓	✓
10 Wreck: Caesar		✓	✓	✓
11 Wreck: B-29 bomber		✓	✓	✓
12 Wreck: North Carolina			✓	✓
13 Reef: South West Breaker			✓	✓
14 Reef: Inbetweenies		✓	✓	✓
15 Wreck: Mary Celestia		✓	✓	✓
16 Wreck: King		✓	✓	✓
17 Reef: Sandy Hole	✓	✓	✓	✓
18 Reef: Hole in the Wall	✓	✓	✓	✓
19 Reef : Shell Hole		✓	✓	✓
20 Wreck: Minnie Breslauer		✓	✓	✓
21 Reef : Hangover Hole	✓	✓	✓	✓

Bermuda Dive Sites

	Good Snorkeling	Novice	Intermediate	Advanced
22 Wreck: Hermes			✓	✓
23 Reef: Tarpon Hole			✓	✓
24 Wreck: Pollockshields	✓	✓	✓	✓
25 Reef: Cathedral			✓	✓
26 Reef: Nassa Point			✓	✓
27 Wreck: Pelinaion			✓	✓
28 Wreck: Zovetto		✓	✓	✓
29 Wreck: Taunton		✓	✓	✓
30 Wreck: Manilla		✓	✓	✓
31 Wreck: Cristóbol Colón			✓	✓
32 Wreck: Madiana			✓	✓
33 Wreck: Grotto Bay Barges	✓	✓	✓	✓
34 Reef: Devil's Hole	✓	✓	✓	✓
35 Reef: Flatts Bridge	✓		✓	✓
36 Wreck: Xing Da			✓	✓

Dive Site Icons

The symbols at the beginning of the dive site descriptions provide a quick summary of some of the following conditions present at the site:

 Good snorkeling or free diving site

 Cave or caverns. Only experienced cave divers should explore inner cave areas.

 Poor or limited visibility possible

 Strong currents likely

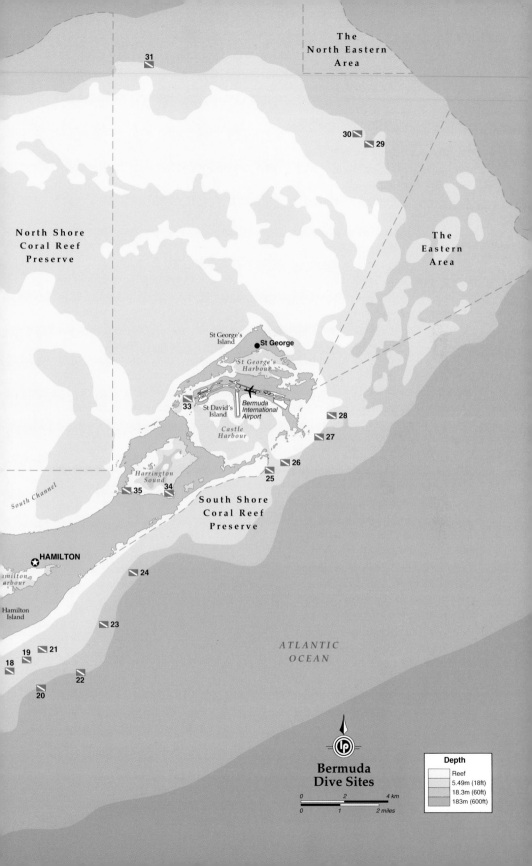

The
North Eastern
Area

31

30 29

North Shore
Coral Reef
Preserve

The
Eastern
Area

St George's
Island

St George

St George's Harbour

33

St David's Island

Bermuda
International
Airport

28

27

Castle
Harbour

26

Harrington
Sound

25

35 34

South Channel

South Shore
Coral Reef
Preserve

HAMILTON

Hamilton
Harbour

24

Hamilton
Island

23

19 21

18

22

20

ATLANTIC
OCEAN

Bermuda
Dive Sites

0   2   4 km
0   1   2 miles

Depth	
	Reef
	5.49m (18ft)
	18.3m (60ft)
	183m (600ft)

1 Reef: Eastern Blue Cut (Blue Hole)

Location: West of Ireland Island

Typical Depth Range: 2-20 meters (6-66 ft)

Typical Current Conditions: Slight

Expertise Required: Intermediate

Access: Boat

Eastern Blue Cut and farther offshore Western Blue Cut are possibly the top dive locations in Bermuda. Although the surrounding area also bears the Western Blue Cut name and includes three wreck sites—*Lartington*, *Constellation* and *Nola*—the dive now known as Eastern Blue Cut or Blue Hole is particularly good. The dive boat drops a sand anchor into a huge sand hole (hence the name "Blue Hole"). Here the boat sits completely sheltered by a surrounding, incredibly beautiful reef. Following the sand slope up the reef edge you will encounter a cave and tunnel system that runs under the reef. This cave usually has several lobsters, but it is not until you emerge onto the outer side of the reef that you will be joined by thousands of silverside minnows.

These tiny silver fish move around you constantly. Although divers are no threat to them, predators such as yellow tail snapper and tuna actively hunt them during daylight hours. One part of the reef is known as Parrot Pass due to the vast numbers of blue parrotfish that constantly move along this gully in the reef. The coral is in excellent condition and the sea fans are particularly healthy. This site is superb for snorkeling, too.

2 Wreck: Constellation

Location: Western Blue Cut

Typical Depth Range: 5-10 meters (16-33 ft)

Typical Current Conditions: Slight to moderate

Expertise Required: Novice

Access: Boat

It was this wreck–and another close by–that inspired Peter Benchley's bestseller, *The Deep*. The *Constellation*, originally named the *Sally Persis Noyes* was built in Harrington, Maine in 1918. This four-masted 60-ft long schooner originally sailed as part of the Crowell and Thurlow fleet. She was eventually sold after years of service to Robert L. Royall in 1932 and renamed the *Constellation*. Royall completely overhauled and rebuilt her, but his plans to transform her into a floating nautical school did not bear fruit, and within a year the ship was sold again.

The Intercontinental Steam Ship Company bought the *Constellation* and oper-ated her from New York. In 1942, during WWII, the demand for ships grew urgent. The *Constellation* was drafted into naval service and was once more converted back into a cargo ship.

In the spring of 1943, she set sail from New York, bound for La Guira, Venezuela,

Most of the *Constellation*'s wreckage lies under the bags of cement she carried as cargo.

on her first voyage after her re-conversion. She carried a general cargo weighing over 2,000 tons, consisting of thousands of bags of cement; 700 cases of Scotch whisky; sheets of plate glass; slate; tennis rackets; lead crucifixes; coffee cups; ceramic tiles; thousands of bottles that contained almost everything from nail polish to mineral water; barrels of cold cream; 400,000 drug ampoules of adrenaline, anti-tetanus, serum, opium, morphine and penicillin; and yo-yo's.

Not long after clearing the New York Roads, she ran into increasingly rough weather and eventually, when her steam-pumping gear broke down, started taking on water. Using only hand pumps, the crew battled in vain to keep her dry. Seventy-one year old Capt. Howard Newes headed for Bermuda for much-needed repairs. On July 30, 1943, while waiting for a pilot to steer her through the treacherous Bermudian reefs to the Royal Naval Dockyard on Ireland Island, she was caught in a powerful current and swept onto the reefs before the pilot could board her. The *Constellation* was a total loss, but the U.S. Navy managed to salvage some of her cargo, including the 700 cases of whisky.

The reefs she struck, in the vicinity of the Western Blue Cut, are renowned for their treachery; in fact the *Constellation* sank only 15 meters away from another, much older ship—at the time thought to be the *Montana,* but now known to be the *Nola.* The *Constellation* is easily found as she is marked by the huge mound of cement bags, now turned to stone. All around, among and under the cement bags, are thousands of broken bottles including—if you are very lucky—some of the now fabled drug ampoules. The position of the Western Blue Cut is marked by a stake and the position of the Eastern Blue Cut is marked by a tripod.

3 Wreck: Nola (Montana)

Location: 15 meters (50 ft) northeast of the Constellation 13 km (8 miles) west of Ireland Island

Typical Depth: 8 meters (25 ft)

Typical Current Conditions: Variable

Expertise Required: Intermediate

Access: Boat

The *Nola* (originally thought to be the *Montana*), an American Civil War blockade runner, was destroyed under very similar conditions to those of the *Constellation*, but much earlier, in 1863. The *Nola* was a 236-ft paddle wheel steamer built by Caird and Sons, Glasgow, around 1862. Displacing 750 tons, she was powered by 260 nominal horse-power twin oscillating cylinder engines. Like her sister ships, the *City of Petersburg* and the *Presto*, the *Nola* was built specifically to run the Union blockade of the Confederate states. To confuse the Union spies, she also sailed under the names *Montana, Gloria* and *Paramount.*

After battling heavy seas, the captain of the *Nola* misjudged the reefs and the strength of the current around the Western Blue Cut–8 miles north-northwest of Ireland Island and the Bermuda dock-yards–and the *Nola* went down.

For the most part, her cargo was completely recovered and was auctioned on behalf of the owners and underwriters at Mangrove Bay in 1864. Sadly the ship did not survive the impact and was unable to be refloated due to the 10-ft gash in her hull. Now she rests in three pieces with her bow relatively intact; although partly collapsed, the paddle wheels are easily discernible, as is the forward boiler, anchor chain and chimney stack.

The *Nola* is extremely photogenic, heavily encrusted in marine growth and surrounded by sergeant majors, yellowtail snapper and chub. It was this wreck and the nearby *Constellation* that inspired Peter Benchley's best-selling book, and later Hollywood film, *The Deep.*

Benchley used the story of drug ampoules near an ancient treasure wreck as the primary plot of the story. Robert Shaw's character, Romer Treece, was based on the world famous Bermudian treasure hunter Teddy Tucker, who acted as consultant on the film in Bermuda. Now both wrecks can be visited quite easily on a single dive. (Incidentally, the other ship mentioned in the film, the *Griffin*, actually came to grief in Bermuda, but much earlier, in 1761. The *Griffin* was an English man-of-war armed with 20 guns. When she struck the reefs of Bermuda on October 25, 50 of her crew drowned.)

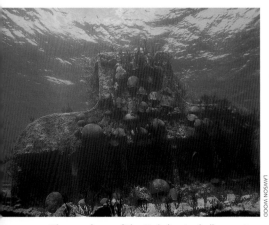

LAWSON WOOD

The wreckage of the *Nola* lies in shallow water.

LAWSON WOOD

Now completely encrusted in colorful marine life, the *Nola* is extremely photogenic.

4 Wreck: Lartington

The *Lartington* was 245-ft long and displaced 878 tons. Built by Short Brothers in Sunderland, England, she was launched in June 1875. Owned by J.S. Barwick, she plied the trade routes between the southern U.S. and Europe, crossing the Atlantic several times in her career.

Location: Near Western Blue Cut
Typical Depth: 9 meters (30 ft)
Typical Current Conditions: Slight to variable
Expertise Required: Novice
Access: Boat

The *Lartington* left Savannah for Russia on December 8, 1878, with a cargo of cotton and under the command of Capt. George Dixon. Soon after leaving port she was struck by a hurricane and all of her deck cargo was washed off. Another storm cracked her timbers and, fearing that the ship would be lost, Capt. Dixon altered course for Bermuda. She struck the reef near the wreck of the *Nola* in the vicinity of Western Blue Cut. All the crew were saved.

The name "Lartington" can still be seen quite clearly on the bow of the ship, her twin boilers lying side-by-side and the propeller shaft leading to a ruined propeller. The *Lartington* is popular with novice divers who can enjoy their first wreck encounter with one that still looks like a ship. Almost all the ship is now heavily encrusted in marine life. The surrounding reef has good coral growth and fish.

Trainee divers near the *Lartington*.

5 Wreck: L'Herminie

L'Herminie was a 300-ft 60 gun French frigate launched in 1828 as part of a fleet of ships sent by France to enforce its claims against Mexico. She had arrived in Havana on August 31, 1837, but in the three months she was stationed there, 133 of her crew came down with yellow fever and it was decided to send the ship back to France because her crew would be useless in battle. Under the command of Com. Bazoche she was bound for Brest, France, when rough weather persuaded Bazoche to seek shelter in Bermudian waters. Sadly, due to her size, she lacked maneuverability and was soon locked within a treacherous reef system, with no way out. *L'Herminie* finally foundered and wrecked on December 4, 1838. All 495 officers and crew were saved and landed at Ely's Harbour, and in the days that followed, salvage operations were successfully carried out.

Location: Near Chub Heads Reef 6 km (4 miles) west of Ireland Island
Typical Depth Range: 8-11 meters (25-36 ft)
Typical Current Conditions: Slight to moderate, swell may be encountered
Expertise Required: Novice/Intermediate
Access: Boat

The ship's hull has long since vanished, but up to 40 of her iron cannons are still clearly visible, including two crossed cannons on the sand, a favorite subject for photographers. The ship's winch is visible as is part of the tiled cookhouse flooring. Other artifacts include cannon balls and a large fluted anchor. The ship's bell was recovered by Teddy Tucker. Nearby is an older wreck's ballast pile, which has fossil teeth among the stones.

The ballast stones from *L'Herminie* are scattered near the wreckage.

6 Reef: Chub Heads

Chub Heads Reef is more commonly associated with the wreck of *L'Herminie*, but the reefs themselves are well worth separate exploration. Continuing southwest from the wreck, the reefs gradually form more complex and densely packed forms. Their convoluted shape creates various large coral heads with numerous swim-throughs, gullies and canyons. Much of the reef structure is overhanging and fringed in soft corals and sea fans. Under the overhangs you will find the warty corallimorph (*Discosoma sanctithomae*), which yields a nasty sting if touched by bare skin. Christmas tree worms *(Spirobranchus giganteus)* are also common.

The predominant type of sea fan is *Gorgonia ventalina,* and the brightly colored Venus sea fan (*Gorgonia flabellum)* is seen as well. If you look closely at the fans, you will more than likely see arrow crabs *(Stenorhynchus seticornis)* or the flamingo

Location: 6 km (4 miles) west of Ireland Island
Typical Depth Range: 8-12 meters (25-40 ft)
Typical Current Conditions: Variable, sea can be choppy and subject to swell
Expertise Required: Intermediate
Access: Boat

tongue shell (*Cyphoma gibbosum).* Small schools of bluehead wrasse (*Thalassoma bifasciatum)* are common everywhere, the groups comprising ten to twenty small yellow fish with a black blotch at the top of the dorsal fin; they will sometimes be accompanied by a "super-male," which is typically larger and has a dark blue head. This is one of the many reef fishes that undergo both sex and color changes. As the name of this reef implies, there are also large schools of Bermuda chub *(Kyphosus sectatrix).*

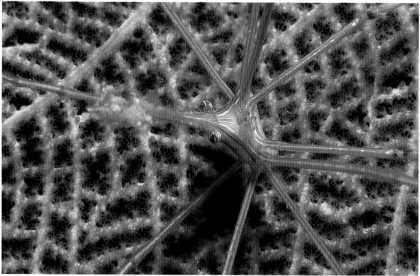

Arrow crabs (*Stenorhynchus seticornis*) are one of the more peculiar-looking reef inhabitants.

7 Wreck: Darlington

The *Darlington* was a steel-hulled English steamer, built in 1881 by Swan Hunter shipyard in Tyneside for W. Milburn and Company of London. She was 285-ft long, displaced 1,990 tons, and was driven by 250-hp compound inverted steam engines. The *Darlington* was wrecked on February 21, 1886 while en route from New Orleans to Bremen, carrying a cargo of cotton and grain.

The accident was caused purely by a navigational miscalculation. Capt. Richard Ward and his first mate were both found negligent by the subsequent board of inquiry and had their certificates of competency revoked. All the *Darlington*'s 23 crew members were saved and returned to New York.

The *Darlington* now rests on her port side, the superstructure collapsed in on itself; the boilers, winches, propeller shaft and huge four-bladed propeller are still clearly visible. Schools of sergeant majors (*Abudefduf saxatilis*) have made their home here and will swarm around you. Look out for clumps of their red-colored eggs, which are attached to the undersides of the metal surfaces. This wreck is an interesting dive for all levels, and nearby are the much older remains of a Spanish galleon, buried in the sand.

Location: 5 km (3 miles) west of West End

Typical Depth Range: 5-9 meters (16-30 ft)

Typical Current Conditions: Slight, but choppy on surface

Expertise Required: Novice/Intermediate

Access: Boat

LAWSON WOOD

Wooden dead heads used on sailing ships to thread ropes for hauling sails are found preserved on the *Darlington*.

8 Reef: Dockyards Snorkel Park

This underwater park is a new addition for snorkelers and is well laid out directly under the walls to the left of the old Bermuda dockyards, which now house the Bermuda Maritime Museum. Seven cast iron cannons have been located in the park, dating from 1550 to 1800. Two are "24 pounders," one a "3 pounder," and four are "2 pounders"—a reference to the weight of the shot. Other artifacts include an 18th century anchor, a 19th century gun-carriage wheel and a large metal barrel. The cannons have been marked by small buoys and you are able to follow a carefully planned route among the shallow coral heads.

Location: West of the Maritime Museum
Typical Depth Range: 1-5 meters (3-20 ft)
Typical Current Conditions: None
Expertise Required: Novice
Access: Beach or small craft

The Dockyards Snorkel Park is a protected reef preserve where you will be able to observe sea anemones, sea cucumbers, tiny crabs, shrimp and more than fifty varieties of fish, many of which are juveniles that have "grown up" within the protective embrace of the shallower reef. There are squirrelfish, wrasse, butterflyfish, trumpetfish, gobies, blennies and pufferfish. Squid and octopus are seen regularly during the evenings, and parrotfish can be observed (and heard) eating corals. As you swim close to the old fort's walls, you will come across pottery shards and musket balls that date from when the fort started construction in 1809, and electrical insulators dating from WWII when the fort was used as a radio station. At Dockyards, you'll find equipment rentals, floating rest stations and lifeguards on duty ☎ 441-234 1006 (beach); 441-292 8652 (office); fax 441-292 5193).

Dockyards Snorkel Park protects a variety of fish including this pipefish nestled in grape algae.

9 Wreck: Vixen

The *Vixen* was built by Lungley shipyard in Deptford, England in 1864 and launched in 1867. She was the very first twin-screwed vessel of the Royal Navy. Her teak hull was clad in iron plate to prevent problems from marine organisms, but this also produced considerable drag on the ship and resulted in her being the slowest ship in the Royal Navy.

Location: West of Daniel's Island, Somerset

Typical Depth Range: 0-8 meters (0-25 ft)

Typical Current Conditions: None

Expertise Required: Novice

Access: Boat

Unfortunately, for the *Vixen* and her sister ship the *Viper*, they were considered too slow for general service and were towed to Bermuda to be used as coastal defense ships. The *Vixen* was subsequently used as a dormitory for dockyard workers and in 1896, her engines and machinery were removed and she was sunk off Daniel's Head, primarily as a prevention against possible attacks by torpedo boats.

The *Vixen* is now a protected wreck site and diving can be done by special permit; however, no permit is needed to snorkel the wreck, which is now home to many species of fish. Due to its accessibility, the wreck is also visited regularly by glass-bottomed boats. She is easily found because her hull still protrudes above the water line and, although now has a broken back, is still largely intact.

The *Vixen* is a popular destination for glass bottom boats and an excellent site for snorkeling.

10 Wreck: Caesar

The English brigantine *Caesar* was built by Cumberland and Company, Durham in 1814. While en route between Shields, Newcastle's main port in Tyneside and Baltimore, she was wrecked on May 17, 1818. Capt. James Richardson was in command of the ship and was held responsible for the ship's plight.

Capt. Richardson and the seven crew were all rescued and part of the cargo was salvaged including spars, masts and rigging. The cargo included medicine bottles, grandfather clock parts, glassware, white, red and black lead oxide; a marble cornice for a church in Baltimore, stoneware flasks decorated with masonic symbols; small kegs of lead shot and grindstones. It is these massive grindstones that still lie where the ship first sank and are vir-

Location: Southwest of the island to the outer limits of the patch reef system near the B-29 bomber and the *North Carolina*

Typical Depth: 10 meters (33 ft)

Typical Current Conditions: Light to moderate, swell can be encountered

Expertise Required: Intermediate

Access: Boat

tually all that is left of the ship.

The *Caesar* was extensively salvaged by Teddy Tucker, who found some particularly fine examples of stoneware and glassware, and removed many of the grindstones to build an ornamental path in his garden. The dive is very photogenic and a small band of blue angelfish (*Holocanthus bermudensis*) have made the grindstones their home.

LAWSON WOOD

Grinding stones from the wreck of the *Caesar* litter the seabed.

11 Wreck: B-29 Bomber

This is a dive on the wreckage of a U.S. B-29 bomber, which took off from the airfield at St. David's sometime during 1961 and crashed into the sea due to a fuel problem. Fortunately, all the crew managed to bail out in time and were saved. The aircraft, although largely intact at first, was subsequently blown up by the U.S. military because it was deemed to be a navigational hazard.

The B-29's wreckage is scattered over a wide area and the reef system it lies on is quite compact with few sand holes. All

Location: Near the *North Carolina*, on the southwestern reefs

Typical Depth Range: 8-13 meters (25-43 ft)

Typical Current Conditions: Variable, can be choppy on surface

Expertise Required: Intermediate

Access: Boat

four propellers can be easily found as can recognizable parts of her wings, fuselage and engines. The reef, in fact, is probably more interesting than the airplane, but the combination of the two make the site well worth visiting.

LAWSON WOOD

Aluminum propellers from the B-29 bomber are easily spotted on the reef.

12 Wreck: North Carolina

Location: Near the B-29 wreck, 8 km (5 miles) from Bermuda on the southwest reefs between Long Bar and Little Bar

Typical Depth Range: 8-11 meters (25-36 ft)

Typical Current Conditions: Variable, can be choppy on surface

Expertise Required: Intermediate

Access: Boat

Little is known of the origins of the *North Carolina*, other than that she was an English barque owned by H. Barber and made frequent calls in Bermuda. She was between 150-200 ft long and carried a general cargo of cotton and bark. The ship was en route from Bermuda to Liverpool when the ship's captain, Alexander Buchan, misjudged the reefs and the ship struck fast on January 1, 1880. On January 27 an attempt was made to refloat the vessel, but during the operation, the ship's anchor broke free and crashed through the hull, forever ending any further salvage efforts.

The *North Carolina* looks very much the classic shipwreck and is one of the favorites for visiting divers. She sits upright on the bottom, her bow and stern are intact and her midsection collapsed; the bowsprit still protrudes out into open water, and is now completely covered in sea fans, plumes and small brain corals.

13 Reef: South West Breaker

Location: Southwest from Gibbs Hill Lighthouse

Typical Depth: 11 meters (36 ft)

Typical Current Conditions: Variable, but surge expected

Expertise Required: Intermediate

Access: Boat

This is one of Bermuda's most memorable reef dives. A huge coral head, over 80 meters in circumference, is cut by a cave/tunnel system that runs all the way through the interior of the reef. Depth averages about 11 meters (36 ft) and visibility is usually in excess of 25 meters (80 ft). At low tide, the surf boils over the top of the reef creating a strong suction that can overpower a careless diver. This reef abounds with fish, soft and hard corals, and purple sea fans.

As you enter the cave on the north side, the huge passageway leads around to the right, then to the left. As you approach the underhang at the far side of the tunnel, you will encounter a large school of dogtooth snapper *(Lutjanus jocu)*, and at least three very large black groupers *(Mycteroperca bonaci)*. These will move casually away from you as you approach them. During the spring months, this entrance to the cave system often houses a vast school of silverside minnows and their attendant tarpon *(Megalops atlanticus)*.

South West Breaker should not to be missed, but, due to the surge, conditions must be almost perfect before a dive boat will venture out this far.

Southwest Breaker is cut by a huge cavern that runs completely through the reef.

14 Reef: Inbetweenies

This reef dive is similar to that of South West Breaker, but without the large cave swim-through. The dive is actually on three "blind" breakers, so called because they show on the surface only when the sea is particularly rough and the surge breaks over the top of them. It is no wonder that so many ships have come to grief in Bermuda.

The reefs are in excellent condition and dive boats are able to moor directly next to the breakers on a mooring buoy. Here you can explore the site at your leisure, because it's shallow enough to allow for a maximum bottom time of at least one hour. You can concentrate on your photography, marine life studies, or just enjoy the pleasure of swimming around some of the healthiest reefs in Bermuda waters.

Over many years, angelfish were hand fed in this location. The effect of the feeding has encouraged several species of angelfish to swim directly up to divers, allowing for superb portrait shots of these exquisitely colored creatures.

Location: Southwest from Gibbs Hill Lighthouse, between South West Breaker and the inner reef

Typical Depth: 11 meters (36 ft)

Typical Current Conditions: Variable, but surge expected

Expertise Required: Novice/Intermediate

Access: Boat

Fish Feeding

Fish feeding is frowned upon by the Department of the Environment, dive operators and the local hospitals. Some divers still insist on feeding fish in certain areas, particularly large grouper and moray eels. The result is that fish automatically assume divers have food and react very aggressively when no food is offered. Fish feeding affects both behavior and eating patterns of fish.

Blue angelfish are an indigenous species in Bermuda.

15 Wreck: Mary Celestia (Mari Celeste)

Location: Southeast, offshore from Gibbs Hill Lighthouse

Typical Depth: 15 meters (50 ft)

Typical Current Conditions: Slight to moderate, but can be choppy on the surface

Expertise Required: Intermediate

Access: Boat

The *Mary Celestia* was another blockade runner that hit the reef near what is now the Sonesta Beach Hotel on September 6, 1864. She arrived in St. George from Liverpool on May 16, 1864, just five months after the *Nola* came to grief in Bermuda. Built by William C. Miller in Liverpool, the 207-ton ship was launched in February 1864. Initially known as the *Bijou*, she was constructed specifically to run the Union blockade in the service of the Crenshaw Brothers Company. Although smaller than the *Nola*, she was well built and considered very fast, equipped with twin oscillating cylinder steam engines and feathering paddlewheels.

She cleared customs in Bermuda, supposedly bound for Nassau in the Bahamas, but was actually en route to Wilmington, North Carolina, her sixth voyage to the Confederate port within four months. On September 6, she left with a cargo of 125 boxes of bacon and 534 boxes registered as "general merchandise," which actually contained ammunition and rifles, as well as other foodstuffs such as corned beef. Under the command of Capt. Sinclair, she made a speedier passage than normal

A paddlewheel from the *Mary Celestia* sits upright in the sand.

Divers can explore the *Mary Celestia* and nearby reef in a single dive.

through the east end channels and proceeded west along south shore. Southeast of Gibbs Hill Lighthouse, John Virgin, the Bermudian pilot, brought the ship in close to shore to allow the owner and himself to go ashore.

Unfortunately, before the pilot and Capt. Sinclair could disembark, the *Mary Celestia* hit a reef and sank within eight minutes. The only life lost was that of the cook, who apparently had been the first to notice that they were too close to the reef. The vessel was a total loss, but part of the cargo was salvaged shortly after by divers and auctioned on behalf of the owners.

Much of her hull is now lost beneath the sand, but part of her bow is visible and bent over to her port side. By far the largest section visible is that of the engineering section amidships, where the two huge boilers, each 16 x 10 ft, lie intact. The top of each boiler is formed into a steam chamber with blow-off valves, and on either side of the adjoining paddlewheel shaft lie her great paddlewheels, which are still clearly visible and covered in all manner of coral growth. A small section of the stern can still be seen almost 30 meters behind the engines and has been identified as part of the rudder head.

The site is popular with divers and photographers and, although there is not much of the wreck to be seen, the remnants are particularly interesting in light of her history. The surrounding reef has a few large gullies and canyons that lead back into the convoluted reef where the dive boat is moored. There are some huge sea fans along this reef, and fish life includes sergeant majors, trumpetfish, snappers, grunts and parrotfish.

16 Wreck: King

The U.S. Navy tugboat *King* was built in South Carolina in 1941. She is 55-ft long, and has a 13-ft beam. Bought and operated in Bermudian waters for several years as a converted treasure salvage vessel, she later saw life as one of Bermuda's earliest dive boats. At the end of her service, she was donated as a dive site and sunk by South Side Scuba, becoming the first ship to be scuttled in recent years in Bermuda as a marine habitat for visiting divers.

The tugboat *King* now sits upright but with a 45° list to starboard. Her stern is in the sand and her bow rests on a coral ledge, pointing out to sea, just a short boat ride from two of Bermuda's dive shops. The wreck is quite small and will take only about 15 minutes to explore

Location: Directly opposite the Southampton Princess Hotel

Typical Depth: 20 meters (66 ft)

Typical Current Conditions: Slight, but can be choppy on the surface

Expertise Required: Novice

Access: Boat

fully, allowing you ample time to discover the wealth of marine life on the surrounding reef. The hard corals that predominate are several species of brain coral (*Diplora spp.*) and star coral (*Monastrea spp.*). On closer inspection of some of the deeper recesses you will also see ridged cactus coral (*Mycetophyllia lamarckiana*), which is an almost fluorescent green. Fish are numerous, but are concentrated more on the wreck than on the reef.

17 Reef: Sandy Hole

This is a popular second dive as part of a two-tank dive package. As the name implies, this is a sandy hole framed by a near-vertical coral reef that winds and twists its way along South Shore forming a barrier reef that no ship has been able to survive. The reef is split into many different sections, and experienced dive boat captains zig and zag their way among these treacherous reefs to bring divers to some amazing locations.

Location: Inshore from the *Hermes* to the inner barrier reef

Typical Depth Range: 2-10 meters (6-33 ft)

Typical Current Conditions: None, but can be choppy seasonally

Expertise Required: Novice

Access: Boat

Here you will find huge green moray eels *(Gymnothorax funebris)*, squirrelfish, groupers, coneys, snappers, grunts and parrotfish. Look out for several types of small seabass called hamlets. The barred hamlet *(Hypoplectrus puella)* and the indigo hamlet *(Hypoplectrus indigo)* are found in these waters. Yellowtail damselfish *(Microspathadon chrysurus)* are quite aggressive as they guard their territories, and you can always find the large purple-tipped anemone *(Condylactis gigantea)*. Look closely among the tentacles of the anemone; you may find a small cleaner shrimp *(Periclimenes anthophilus)*, which is one of the few endemic marine species in Bermuda. It can sometimes be seen removing parasites from other reef fishes, but will hide within the anemone's protective embrace when threatened.

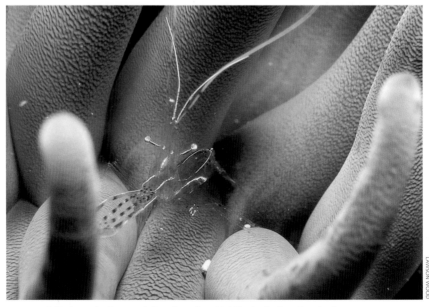

LAWSON WOOD

A Pederson's cleaner shrimp found amidst the tentacles of a giant anemone.

18 Reef: Hole in the Wall

The entire inner ring of this barrier reef along South Shore is remarkable. Here the reef has been sculpted over the centuries by wind and tide into vast domes of coral, each with numerous interconnected caves, gullies, caverns and swim-throughs. One of the most spectacular sites has formed by several large, ancient coral sections "welded" together at the top making a jagged "hole in the wall," which you can swim through easily and is excellent for photography.

Location: Farther east along from Sandy Hole, Warwick Long Bay

Typical Depth Range: 2-12 meters (6-40 ft)

Typical Current Conditions: None, but can experience surge

Expertise Required: Novice/Intermediate

Access: Boat

You can descend down steep sand chutes and into another cave, before you rise to another entrance. Be aware that you can easily lose your bearings in these tunnels, but the surface is never far away and you can always come up and re-orient yourself with the moored dive boat. Compasses are useful in open water, but useless in dead-end gullies and twisting tunnels. Another attraction of this site are the barracudas, tarpons, and schools of large snappers usually present. The shaded areas of the reef are home to some very intricate and brightly colored sponges, anemones and crustaceans, including the banded coral shrimp (*Stenopus hispidus*).

19 Reef: Shell Hole

Location: Farther out into the open reef system from the *King*

Typical Depth: 20 meters (66 ft)

Typical Current Conditions: None, can experience surge in the spring

Expertise Required: Novice

Access: Boat

Shell Hole is another popular reef site and, as the name implies, is well known for the many shells found in the area. Here you can still find the protected flame helmet (*Cassis flammea*), and the Atlantic deer cowrie (*Cypraea cervus*) as well as milk conch, or harbor conch (*Strombus costatus*). Flamingo tongues (*Cyphoma gibbosum*) are common on many of the sea fans.

This is a thriving coral community with most of the species found in this region represented around the perimeter of the natural amphitheatre. You can find gorgonian sea fans, sea plumes and rods, hard and stony corals, all of which provide habitat to numerous varieties of fish including one of the largest of the wrasse species, the puddingwife (*Halichoeres radiatus*), which is forever following divers around. Yellowhead wrasse (*Halichoeres garnoti*) are also common as well as Spanish hogfish (*Bodianus rufus*) and foureye butterflyfish (*Chaetodon capistratus*).

20 Wreck: Minnie Breslauer

The *Minnie Breslauer* was a 300 ft-long English steamer launched in December 1872. En route from Portugal to New York on her maiden voyage, she carried a cargo of dried fruit, wine, cork and lead. The steamer was powered by a 260-horsepower single oscillating cylinder steam engine and was under the command of Capt. Peter Corbett. Like so many other sea captains before (and after) him, Corbett decided to use Bermuda as a landmark before turning northwest to New York.

Completely misjudging his position with respect to the Bermudian reefs, Capt. Corbett ran the ship aground on the

Location: Between Horseshoe Bay and Warwick Long Bay

Typical Depth Range: 12-21 meters (40-70 ft)

Typical Current Conditions: Variable, but can be choppy on the surface

Expertise Required: Novice/Intermediate

Access: Boat

southern shoals. The *Minnie Breslauer* was later pulled off those reefs and an attempt was made to tow her up to St. George for repairs at the shipyard. The damage was so great, however, that she soon started to take in water and sank off South Shore. All her crew was saved and much of her cargo salvaged by the agents for the shipping

LAWSON WOOD

Shipwrecks, like the *Minnie Breslauer*, attract a wide variety of marine life and provide endless opportunities for diver exploration.

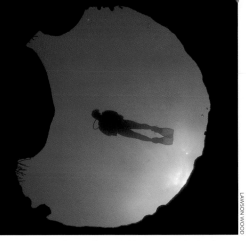

A diver sillouetted by a porthole on the
Minnie Breslauer.

line. Not all of the cargo was salvaged, however, and ten days after her sinking a warning was posted that anyone found in possession of cargo would be prosecuted.

The ship's bow is completely smashed and well embedded into the coral reef. Between her amidships and stern, much of the ship is still relatively intact, including the machinery of the engine and the large single steam boiler, which sits upright against the reef. The engine shape is very similar to that of the *Nola* and the *Lart-*

ington. The remainder of her superstructure is well spread out on a sandy bottom and you can still find her propeller and chimney stack.

Much of the metalwork of the ship has collapsed, and round holes where the portholes used to be make for an interesting photographic frame when looking up at divers passing overhead. There are no shallow reefs breaking the surface in this area, so dive boats are able to moor directly over the wreck, making for an easy and comfortable dive.

The *Minnie Breslauer* is now well encrusted in soft and hard corals of many different varieties. There are usually chub, sergeant majors and yellowtail snappers nearby, and on the sandy floor around the ship you can usually see sand divers *(Synodus intermedius)* and peacock flounders *(Bothus lunatus)*. Plumed scorpionfish *(Scorpaena grandicornis)*, although considered very rare, can often be seen among the wreckage, lying in wait for a passing morsel of food.

Peacock flounders are found camouflaged in turtle grass on the sandy seabed.

21 Reef: Hangover Hole

Its dramatic tunnels and archways make dropping into Hangover Hole's narrow clefts exciting, and the many small caves and swim-throughs provide a superb backdrop for photography and observing marine life. One deep cave in particular has several small shafts of light that bisect the gloom, and there you can find a small school of glassy sweepers *(Pempheris schomburgki)*. Spotted drum *(Equetus puntatus)* can also be found under these overhangs as well as various species of groupers, wrasse, snappers, parrotfish and grunts.

Location: Next section east from Hole in the Wall dive site

Typical Depth Range: 3-13 meters (10-43 ft)

Typical Current Conditions: None in tunnels, surge often on surface

Expertise Required: Novice/Intermediate

Access: Boat

Several of the larger overhangs have a resident group of dog-toothed snappers *(Lutjanus jocu)* as well as schoolmasters *(Lutjanus apodus)* and yellowtail snappers *(Ocyurus chrysurus)*. Rock beauties *(Holacanthus tricolor)* are evident, as are other angelfish. Arrow crabs *(Stenorhynchus seticornis)* are fairly common, as are spiny lobsters *(Panulirus argus)*. Overall, this is a superb reef dive with plenty to keep everyone happy, and a favorite with the dive shops because it is such a short boat trip.

This juvenile spotted drum "dances" at the entrance to its shelter under the reef.

22 Wreck: Hermes (Fogo Brava)

Location: 1km off Warwick Long Bay

Typical Depth: 22 meters (72 ft)

Typical Current Conditions: Slight, but can be choppy on the surface

Expertise Required: Intermediate/Advanced

Access: Boat

The *Hermes* is a 254-ton 165-ft-long freighter built in Pennsylvania in 1943. She was originally a U.S. Navy buoy tender and used to transport light goods—until she broke down, was towed to and later abandoned in Bermuda, because the new owners could not afford to pay for her repair costs. After some unsuccessful attempts to sell the ship, the government eventually donated the *Hermes* to the Bermuda Divers Association (BDA). She was stripped and cleaned at Dockyard, all her hatches removed, and was scuttled on May 15, 1984, instantly becoming one of the most popular dive sites along the south shore.

Unlike the other Bermudian shipwrecks, the *Hermes* is completely intact and sits upright in a sandy hole wedged between two very interesting sections of reef. The ship is easily penetrated and divers are able to explore the cargo hold, captain's quarters, and engine room with twin diesel six-cylinder engines. The mast still stands intact and is now home to numerous sergeant majors, parrotfish and snappers. Gradually, the hull is being covered in a fine film of coral and algae growth and becomes more photogenic with each passing year.

LAWSON WOOD

The *Hermes* is completely open, allowing for safe access to all her parts, including the engine room pictured here.

23 Reef: Tarpon Hole

Tarpon Hole is another favorite dive site of many operators. It's a little farther from the dive centers than normal, but well worth the extra journey time. The reef has evolved into strange convoluted shapes with some simply massive overhangs, swim-throughs, caves and tunnels. You never know what is around the next corner and you can swim from cave to cave without emerging onto the outer reef.

Location: East of the *Pollockshields* next to a large "boiler reef"
Typical Depth Range: 3-12 meters (10-40 ft)
Typical Current Conditions: Slight, but can have strong surge on the surface
Expertise Required: Intermediate
Access: Boat

The site is named after the tarpons *(Megalops atlanticus)* that return year after year to drift in canyons and secluded areas during the day, forming small schools of perhaps 20 to 30 individuals. At night, they leave the protection of the inner reef

LAWSON WOOD

Convolutions in the reef at Tarpon Hole make it a favorite site for divers.

and roam the reefs as aggressive predators. You will also find dog-toothed snapper (*Lutjanus jocu*) and a few porkfish (*Anisotremus virginicus*) inhabiting the same space under the overhang at the entrance to the largest cave.

During the summer months, schools of silverside minnows congregate in the area and when they move in, the tarpon will feed during the day, rounding the fish up in the shallower areas and attacking with great precision.

24 Wreck: Pollockshields

The *Pollockshields*, originally named the *Herodot*, was built by Reiherstieg Schiffswerft, Hamburg for Deutsche Dampfs in 1890. She was 323-ft long, and displaced 2,744 gross tons, and was powered by 281 horsepower triple expansion engines. She was sold in 1903 to the Hamburg American Shipping Line and renamed the *Graecia*. With the outbreak of WWI, she was outfitted as a German naval supply ship. In 1914, while sailing from New York to the Azores, she was captured by the British ship *H.M.S. Argonaut*, renamed the *Pollockshields*, and registered by Tyack & Branfoot in Newcastle.

Location: Directly in front of the Elbow Beach Hotel

Typical Depth Range: 2-9 meters (6-30 ft)

Typical Current Conditions: Slight, but often strong surge

Expertise Required: Novice

Access: From Elbow Beach or by dive boat

En route from Wales to Bermuda in 1915, she was carrying shells, gunpowder and ammunition to support the garrison on Bermuda in case of naval attack. Near the end of her journey she ran into dense fog and hurricane-force winds, and plowed onto the reef in front of Elbow Beach, where the present hotel is situated.

Guests at the hotel and locals, using an old whaling boat, managed to row the 1,500 ft distance five times to rescue the 36 crewmen; Capt. Ernest Boothe, however, was lost early in the rescue attempt.

Until 1960, the wreckage of the *Pollockshields* was stuck fast above the reef, slowly deteriorating and visible to everyone. Teddy Tucker dynamited the ship because it was a hazard to swimmers. Now the ship is scattered over a wide area, but live shells and ammunition can still be found among the coral encrusted wreckage. A recent survey by the Royal Navy has declared that the ship may be unsuitable for divers due to ammunition still present, but it is still easily accessible from the beach to snorkelers.

To visit all of the wreck site, you must cross the reef crest into the shallower water of the inner reef, but there is generally always a strong surge over the reef and you must exercise great care when attempting this. The reef area is still largely spoiled due to the explosives, but it is slowly growing back, and much of the ferrous metal surfaces are being colonized. Sergeant majors (*Abudefduf saxatilis*) and princess parrotfish (*Scarus taeniopterus*) are the most common fish found around the wreck site. If you do come across any ammunition, whether it looks live or not, *leave it alone.*

25 Reef: Cathedral

Near Gurnet Rock off the East End and a favorite for the dive shops at this end of the island, the Cathedral is well named. It is a huge underwater dome with several "windows" where shafts of light penetrate into the gloom, giving a feeling of being inside a vast subterranean cathedral.

Location: Near Gurnet Rock
Typical Depth Range: 9-14 meters (30-45 ft)
Typical Current Conditions: Slight, but often strong surge
Expertise Required: Intermediate
Access: Boat

You can always find interesting sponges, low encrusting corals and schools of small fish all around the area. Look out for the masked or glass goby *(Coryphopterus personatus/hyalinus)* on the star corals and the bridled goby *(Coryphopterus glaucofraenum)* among the sand and coral rubble. Bandtail puffer *(Sphaeroides spengleri)* are fairly common, as are the usual snappers, parrotfish, squirrelfish and small groupers. This is a very popular dive with a high concentration of marine life.

Also found in the immediate area around the entrances to Castle Harbour are the wrecks of the *Kate, Cerberus, Warwick* and *Katherine*. Nearby Nonsuch Island is where William Beebe launched his bathysphere to explore the deep escarpment that surrounds Bermuda. A replica of the bathysphere is on exhibit at the Bermuda Aquarium.

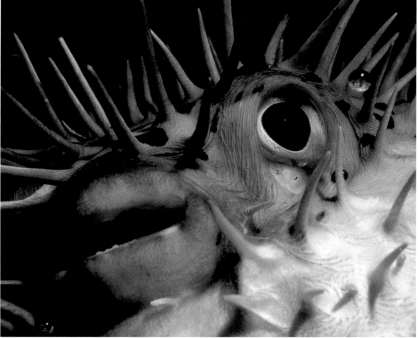

LAWSON WOOD

The shy pufferfish should never be handled as it will inflate in defense and lose the protective mucus coating on its skin.

26 Reef: Nassa Point

The visibility in the vicinity of East End and opposite the entrance to Castle Harbour is reduced due to the dredging and construction of the airport at St. David's. Here you'll see fewer of the large sea fans and smaller hard corals because the sedimentation is not favored by those species. There are some excellent soft corals, sea whips and plumes, however, which are better able to tolerate these conditions.

Location: Out from the Cathedral dive site to next line of breakers near Cooper's Island

Typical Depth Range: 9-15 meters (30-50 ft)

Typical Current Conditions: Slight, but strong surge

Expertise Required: Intermediate

Access: Boat

The reduced visibility does not detract from the popularity of the area because there are numerous caverns, swim-throughs and gullies to explore. This site has several huge overhangs that are similar to the Hangover Hole dive. Tarpon *(Megalops atlanticus)* hang out here during the winter months; in the summer, their position is taken by dog-toothed snapper *(Lutjanus jocu)* and the gray snapper *(Lutjanus griseus)*. Sergeant majors and yellowhead wrasse are common on the reef crest and you will almost always see parrotfish and surgeonfish.

LAWSON WOOD

27 Wreck: Pelinaion

The Greek steamer *Pelinaion,* built in 1907 by Russel and Company, Port Glasgow for Hill SS Company, was first known as the *Hill Glen.* She was 385-ft long, displaced 4,291 gross tons and was powered by 384 horsepower triple expansion engines. During the next 22 years, she was sold several times and was known as the *Doonholm,* the *Ktistakis K,* and finally as the *Pelinaion.*

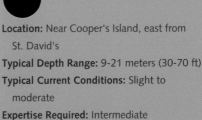

Location: Near Cooper's Island, east from St. David's

Typical Depth Range: 9-21 meters (30-70 ft)

Typical Current Conditions: Slight to moderate

Expertise Required: Intermediate

Access: Boat

She left Takiradi in West Africa bound for Baltimore, Maryland on December 22, 1939 with a cargo of manganese ore. Capt. Volikas did not know that the lighthouse at St. David's had been blacked out due to the war, and on January 16, 1940, he entered Bermuda waters for the last time. The currents around Cooper's Island can be notoriously strong, unfortunately for Capt. Volakis, an experienced captain, he ran aground and the ship was wrecked.

The *Pelinaion* is now completely broken up. She had four massive boilers, two of which are on the reef top, the others on the sand. Huge mounds of anchor chain can be seen as well as winches, propeller and anchors. This convoluted reef is also excellent for exploration.

28 Wreck: Zovetto (Rita Zovetta)

The *Zovetto*, originally known as the *War Gascon*, was built by A. Stephen & Sons Ltd. of Glasgow in 1919. She was almost 400-ft long and displaced 5,107 gross tons. Sold to Parodi & Accame of Genoa, she was renamed the *Zovetto*.

Like the *Pelinaion*, the *Zovetto* was a manganese ore carrier and was en route from Gibraltar to Baltimore when she entered Bermuda waters on February 11, 1924. Under direction from a Bermuda pilot boat, Capt. Fortunat de Gregari somehow misinterpreted the pilot's signals

Location: North of the *Pelinaion*, opposite St. David's Island

Typical Depth Range: 6-21 meters (20-70 ft)

Typical Current Conditions: Slight to moderate, surge common

Expertise Required: Novice/Intermediate

Access: Boat

and due to the very rough seas at the time, missed the channel and ran aground near St. David's Lighthouse. Fortunately for Capt. Fortunat, no lives were lost and the cargo was subsequently recovered.

Bluehead and creole wrasse constantly move over the reef, eating algae.

LAWSON WOOD

By far the most interesting part of the dive is the intact stern section, where you can find the massive propeller, which is missing two blades. The rest of the wreckage is scattered over a wide area and although covered in sparse coral growth, it is more interesting for the marine life and the numbers of parrotfish and wrasse that can be seen feeding around the hulking remains.

29 Wreck: Taunton

The *Taunton* was built in Copenhagen in 1902 by Burmeister & Wain and sailed under Norwegian registry, owned by A.F. Kaceness & Co. She was 230-ft long and displaced 1,329 gross tons, powered by a triple expansion engine.

En route from Norfolk, Virginia to St. George in Bermuda with a cargo of coal and under the command of Capt. Olsen, she was making "heavy weather" in a dense fog on November 24, 1920, when she was wrecked on the shallow reefs near the northeast breakers. The *Taunton* lies in an area that is also the graveyard of several other ships: the *Eagle*; *Manilla*; *Iristo*; *Elda*; *Cristóbol Colón* and the *Curlew*. (These are the more documented sites, there are also pieces of wooden wreckage and ballast stones from many much older wrecks, the true identities of which have not been identified yet.)

Location: Near North East Breakers

Typical Depth Range: 3-12 meters (10-40 ft)

Typical Current Conditions: Variable, but strong surge and surface chop common

Expertise Required: Novice/Intermediate

Access: Boat

The wreckage of the *Taunton* is now broken up and scattered over a very wide area. The bow is still relatively intact and very photogenic, completely covered in small brain corals and sea fans. The site is popular as a second dive due to its shallow depth. Look for the Victorian "head" (toilet cubicle), separate from the wreckage near the bow section. The engine and boiler are still discernible, but the rest of the wreck is completely scattered. The bell was discovered by Teddy Tucker and used as a prop in the film *The Deep*.

30 Wreck: Manilla (Ginger Beer Bottle)

Known as the *Manilla* wreck or sometimes the *Ginger Beer Bottle* wreck, this former Dutchman was wrecked on the northeastern reefs around the mid-18th century. Historical records show that a Dutch or Danish ship of unknown character was wrecked in the vicinity in 1753; others attribute this wreck as the *Lord Frederick*, an English merchantman sailing from the Clyde in Scotland to

Location: Close by the Taunton dive site and can be reached on same dive

Typical Depth: 5 meters (16 ft)

Typical Current Conditions: Variable, but strong surge common due to shallow depth

Expertise Required: Novice/Intermediate

Access: Boat

Charleston, South Carolina. Still others reckon she was a privateering vessel, due to the discoveries of various artifacts and the many large iron guns that are embedded in the shallow reef.

Artifacts discovered include tiny glass beads, bronze "slave" bangles, stone ginger beer bottles, clay pipe bowls and stems, pottery and glassware. The wreck is protected and privately owned by Harry Cox, who has researched many of Bermuda's wrecks. This is a shallow reef area with another three wrecks within the immediate vicinity and care should be taken due to the frequent surge. This stretch of coral reef is the most northerly coral reef in the world, fed by the warm waters of the Gulf Stream. There is a profusion of soft and hard corals and schools of wrasse, parrotfish and snapper all over the reef.

31 Wreck: Cristóbol Colón

Built in 1923 for the Transatlantica Spanish Line in El Ferrol, the Spanish liner *Cristóbol Colón* is Bermuda's largest shipwreck. Bound for Vera Cruz in Mexico from Wales, she was 500-ft long and displaced almost 11,000 tons. Although she was supposedly carrying no passengers, there was a suspiciously large number of crew members—160 plus six stewardesses—under the command of Capt. Crescencia Narvarro Delgado. Steaming at 15 knots on

Location: Among the northern reefs near North Rock

Typical Depth Range: 9-17 meters (30-55 ft)

Typical Current Conditions: Variable

Expertise Required: Intermediate

Access: Boat

October 25, 1936, she plowed into the reef near North Rock, 8 miles north of Bermuda Dockyard.

It was thought at the time that the ship had been used by the Spanish Loyalists

LAWSON WOOD

Covered in small brain coral, the *Cristóbol Colón* is now spread over a wide area of reef.

LAWSON WOOD

The *Cristóbol Colón*'s winches, drive shaft and anchors are still evident.

during the Spanish Civil War to travel to Cuba to collect arms for their cause and to smuggle out high ranking officials from Spain to Havana. Unfortunately for all concerned, not only was the ship wrecked, but three months after the accident all "crew members" were returned to Spain. Handsomely outfitted, much of the *Cristóbol Colón* was salvaged and auctioned in St. George in March 1941.

The wreck is now lying well broken up in two distinct sections split by a large section of coral reef. Divers can find eight boilers, two massive propshafts and propellers, winches and gears, all becoming heavily encrusted in marine growth.

32 Wreck: Madiana

The *Madiana* was a passenger liner built by R. Napier & Sons, Glasgow in 1877. Originally known as the *Balmoral Castle*, she was almost 345-ft long, displaced over 3,000 gross tons and was powered by 383 horsepower triple expansion engines. In the years to come she changed names another two times, finally being renamed the *Madiana* when she was sold to Quebec Steam Ship Company of Montreal.

Location: 5 km west of North Rock

Typical Depth: 11 meters (36 ft)

Typical Current Conditions: Variable, but can be surge and surface chop

Expertise Required: Intermediate

Access: Boat

Just before Valentine's Day in 1903, the ship was threading her way through the reefs to the northeast of Bermuda, en route to Hamilton. Unfortunately for

Capt. Roderick Frazer, the Gibbs Hill Lighthouse was malfunctioning and he mistook its light for another, subsequently crashing into the reef during the heavy rolling sea. All passengers and crew were saved.

The ship is now completely broken up and is easily explored in the shallow water. Dive boats anchor in a sand hole near the stern of the ship. From there you can follow the massive raised propeller shaft to the twin boilers lying on their sides. The boilers have huge holes all of the way through, which are home to countless sergeant majors and other damselfish. The wreck of the *Caraquet*, sunk in 1923, lies nearby.

LAWSON WOOD

The wreck of the *Madiana* is now completely encrusted in both hard and soft coral.

33 Reef: Grotto Bay Barges

There is no official reference to the Grotto Bay barges, but the area was used as a marine dump at the end of WWII. The barges are reputed to have been scuttled deliberately, though not intended as the diving attraction they are now. These barges sit upright in a sheltered bay with little tidal movement; the area suffers from poor visibility compared to normal Bermuda standards. Favored as an easy site for students, the barges are considered a good location for night diving.

Location: In front of Grotto Bay Hotel, next to the causeway

Typical Depth: 5 meters (16 ft)

Typical Current Conditions: None, but reduced visibility

Expertise Required: Novice

Access: The jetty at Grotto Bay

Leaving the end of the dock at Grotto Bay, you'll reach the barges after a short swim over a flat sandy seabed covered in an algal "fuzz." You commonly see peacock flounders *(Bothus lunatus)*, plumed scorpionfish *(Scorpaena grandicornis)* and box crabs *(Calappa gallus)*. The underside of the ships' hulks have a resident

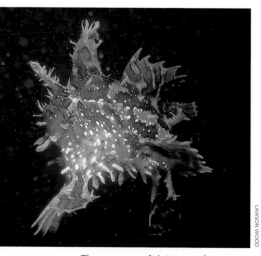

The sargassumfish is one of
Bermuda's rarest visitors.

population of spiny lobsters *(Panulirus argus)* and the much smaller guinea-chick lobster *(Panulirus guttatus)*.

You can easily spend hours exploring these hulks and you will always encounter interesting invertebrates, small corals, tunicates, brilliantly colored sponges. If you're lucky, you may see some of the rarest creatures found in Bermudian waters—the longsnout seahorse *(Hippocampus reidi)* and the sargassumfish *(Histrio histrio)*, incredibly exciting finds for the diver and underwater photographer.

34 Reef: Devil's Hole

Devil's Hole is an especially good dive site for observing some of the many species of marine life not normally associated with the outer reefs. The creatures here prefer calm, sheltered locations away from the constant threat of storm and reef predators. The site also makes an excellent night dive.

The area around the shoreline at Devil's Hole is particularly interesting because of the number of openings into the underwater caves and caverns, typical of those found in this section of Bermuda. However, *do not enter or explore these caves unless you are specially trained in cave diving, and have permission from the Bermuda Tourism Office.* Many of the caves are interconnected and very narrow, it is quite possible to become hopelessly—and dangerously—lost in them. The entrances to the caverns are home to many creatures fairly rare to Bermuda, such as the berried anemone *(Alicia mirabilis)*, the brilliantly colored

Location: Bottom of Knapton Hill Rd., at the corner of Harrington Sound
Typical Depth: 3 meters (10 ft)
Typical Current Conditions: None
Expertise Required: Novice/Intermediate
Access: From the shore next to the jetty

banded coral shrimp *(Stenopus hispidus)*, lightbulb tunicates *(Clavelina picta)*, red night shrimp *(Rhynchocinetes rigens)*. If you're lucky you might spot the very rare sea urchin shrimp *(Gnathophylloides mineri)*, which hides among the spines and tube feet of the sea urchin *(Tripneustes ventricosus)*, and the brightly colored squat anemone shrimp *(Thor amboinensis)*. This site is superb for macro photography because of the calm, shallow water directly off the shore where you are not limited by time or dive boat constraints.

35 Reef: Flatts Bridge

Of all the dive sites in Bermuda, the Flatts Bridge site is at the top of many divers' lists. You must dive the site during slack water—2 hours and 20 minutes after the published time of high and low tide each day, when you have up to 20 minutes of relative calm. My recommendation is to spend some time snorkeling on the periphery of the tidal race before slack water, and as the current slackens, start to enter into the tidal stream at an angle. On the inside of Harrington Sound, which is a protected marine preserve, the lip of the mini-wall is horseshoe-shaped and steeply undercut. Once you reach this area, you will be completely protected from any current overhead. The underhangs have more blue angelfish than in any other dive site in Bermuda, as well as massive lobster.

Location: Harrington Sound/Flatts Village inlet, next to the Bermuda Aquarium, Museum and Zoo

Typical Depth Range: 2-9 meters (6-30 ft)

Typical Current Conditions: During tidal shifts, 3.5 knot currents expected; dives should be made at slack water

Expertise Required: Intermediate

Access: From the concrete bridge platform on the Flatts Village side of the bridge on the Harrington Sound side

Gradually, the current diminishes as the tide slackens, and you can then emerge from the protection of the wall and explore the shallow area underneath the bridge. You'll see huge areas of red sponge interspersed with green feather algae

Flatts Bridge is possibly the best shore dive in Bermuda, but watch out for boat traffic!

(*Caulerpa sertularoides*) and green grape algae (*Caulerpa racemosa*), as well as tube worms, crabs, anemones, shrimps and lobsters.

If you pass all the way under the bridge into the marina at Flatts Village, you'll probably see numerous old glass bottles and jars, all of which have been covered in a film of fire coral (*Millepora alcicornis*). Here in this sheltered marina you can also find the longsnout seahorse (*Hippocampus reidi*) on the mooring chains and lines. Pipefish (*Sygnathus pelagicus*) and longspine squirrelfish (*Holocentrus rufus*) are also common amid the grape algae stems.

One hazard you may encounter during slack water is that boat traffic might be heavy, particularly at the high-tide slack water. Watch out for boats and stay out of their way when diving in this area. At the high tide slacks, I prefer to explore the periphery of the shoreline on the Flatts Village side of Harrington Sound. There are several large coral boulders here, which break the surface; underneath them are hundreds of guinea-chick lobsters. Most of the old coralline limestone surfaces are covered in bright red sponges, with attendant starfish (*Asterinopsis pilosa*) and small blennies (*Scartella cristata*).

Although Flatts Bridge can be difficult due to the strength of the tidal race, the effort involved is well worth it. The photographic possibilities are superb, and you have a greater-than-average chance of seeing some large pelagics, such as rays, which pass to and from the sound.

36 Wreck: Xing Da

In October 1996, the 221-ft merchant vessel *Xing Da* was seized in Bermuda waters after the U.S. Coastguard and Marines discovered that she was carrying 80 illegal Chinese immigrants. (Incidentally, the name *Xing Da* means "Lucky Ride.") This was the third such trip for this ship, which carried passengers paying up to $30,000 each to be smuggled into the U.S. A search for the rightful owner of the ship proved futile. Under the coordination of Michael Burke, owner of Blue Water Divers, the Bermuda Diving Association acquired the ship, and with the help of the government, thoroughly cleaned of all her oil and fuel wastes. Now safe for diver penetration, the *Xing Da* was scuttled on May 15, 1997, in 100-ft of water off the Eastern Blue Cut.

Location: North of the Dockyard to the outer northwest reefs near Eastern Blue Cut

Typical Depth: 27 meters (90 ft)

Typical Current Conditions: Very slight, but can be choppy on the surface

Expertise Required: Intermediate

Access: Boat

The authorities had intended to sink the ship in a specific sandhole, but as she sank, the ship shifted and about one-third of her length landed on the reef with minimal damage. The ship is already home to a wide variety of fish species, including snapper, that have made this new artificial reef their home. Now explored as a two-tank dive, the *Xing Da* is a welcome addition to the local dive scene.

Marine Life of Bermuda

LAWSON WOOD

Classification and Nomenclature

In this guidebook, both the common names and the scientific (Latin) names of local species are given. Scientific names are useful because the same common name is often applied to different species in different parts of the world. Scientific names for living things use the following convention: the first name is the genus to which it belongs, and the first letter is capitalized. This is followed by its specific (species) name, which starts with a lowercase letter (i.e., *Holacanthus bermudensis*). Once you get into the habit of using the proper scientific name, you'll soon find how useful it is to describe species in a common language understood world-wide.

Overview of Bermuda Marine Life

Approximately 10,000 species of marine life have been recorded in Bermuda waters. Following is a brief summary of the most common groups of plants and animals you will encounter around the Bermuda islands.

Invertebrate Animals   Most marine animals are invertebrates–or animals without backbones. Bermuda, swept by the nutrient rich waters from the Gulf Stream, is visited by a high proportion of the species found in the nearby ocean.

The **Porifera**, or sponges, are considered the most primitive and simple of all animals. In Bermuda, they are usually small, encrusting, brightly colored and found in shaded areas attached to rocks and corals. They tend to be most abundant where the water is swiftly moving, such as at Flatts Bridge and Somerset Bridge.

Ringed anemone have a symbiotic relationship with several species of shrimp.

The **Cnidaria** (formerly called **Coelenterata**) include a diversity of relatively simple animals. Two different major life-styles occur within this group: attached, such as anemones, and free swimming, such as jellyfish. The moon jellyfish (*Aurelia aurita*) is one of the few local creatures found in every world ocean. A characteristic feature of cnidarians are *nematocysts* –specialized stinging cells used for defense, and/or to paralyze prey. Many cnidarians such as corals or stinging hydroids (*Macrorhynchia spp.*) are not solitary (like anemones), but rather exist as colonies of hundreds or thousands of individuals. The soft corals (*Alcyonaria*) have flexible skeletons, while the hard corals (*Scleractina*) possess rigid, calcareous skeletons.

The moon jellyfish *Aurelia aurita* is found in every world ocean.

Two species of coral compete for space on the same reef.

The largest of the hard, reef-building corals found in Bermuda waters is the boulder star coral (*Monastrea annularis*). Individual colonies may grow to 3 meters or more in diameter. Also common are the brain corals (e.g. *Diplora spp.*), typically attaining widths of 1 meter or so. Soft corals are profuse, and some species of sea fans are much larger here than species found elsewhere in the Caribbean region. The most common soft corals here are sea whips, sea plumes and sea fans, all of which come in many varieties. Among the more predominant species are the common sea fan (*Gorgonia ventalina*) and the venus sea fan (*Gorgonia flabellum*).

Anemones of Bermuda come in many different shapes and sizes. The giant anemone (*Condylactis gigantea*) is perhaps the most common on all of the reefs and has quite long greenish tentacles, often with a purple tip. As with many of the larger anemones in Bermuda, this species often forms symbiotic relationships with a number of other species, including shrimps and crabs. Other common species include the corkscrew anemone (*Bartholomea annulata*) and the related warty corallimorph (*Discosoma sanctithomae*).

Segmented worms (**Annelida**) also display a variety of life-styles. Some wander freely (motile), while others are sedentary, often living in tubes of lime, sand or parchment-like material, which they make themselves and enlarge as they grow. A group known as the **polychaetes** are perhaps the most common of these creatures. The beauty of them all is the Christmas tree worm (*Spirobranchus giganteus*). This worm comes in a multitude of different colors and is often seen rapidly moving down its tube in the coral when you swim close to it.

A cleaning goby shelters under a
Christmas tree worm.

The spiny lobster (*Panulirus argus*) is common on Bermuda's outer reefs.

The **Arthropoda** include the largest number of species of any group in the animal kingdom. These have segmented bodies, external skeletons, and numerous, jointed limbs. Most arthropods, including insects, spiders, centipedes (and their relatives) are strictly terrestrial. One group however, the **crustaceans** (water fleas, barnacles, sand hoppers, shrimps, prawns, lobsters, hermit crabs and many species of true crabs), is aquatic, with the vast majority of its members entirely marine. Among the more common local members of this group are the banded coral shrimp (*Stenopus hispidus*), a small, colorful animal with long pincers. The red hinge-back shrimp (*Rhynchocinetes rugulosa*) can usually be spotted at night by its bright green reflective eyes, and is often found in the shaded areas beneath granite boulders. Other common small shrimps include *Thor amboinensis* and

The rare periclemines shrimp can be seen among the spines and tentacles of this sea urchin.

Periclimenes anthophilus, both of which are found on anemones. Slipper lobsters and spiny lobsters inhabit the reef ledges. Perhaps most comical of all crustaceans are hermit crabs, such as the orangeclaw hermit (*Calcinus tibicen*). This animal is quite wary of divers, and will readily retreat into its mobile home.

The **Mollusca** also exhibit considerable variety, and include bivalves (clams, mussels, scallops), snails, chitons and octopus. Marine forms of the gastropoda (limpets, periwinkles and snails) usually have a one-piece shell and are benthic in habitat (living on the sea floor); although a few with greatly reduced shells swim near the surface. The bivalve molluscs have a shell composed of more or less equal halves. The cephalopods (squid, octopus) are the most highly advanced members of this group and are swift, intelligent predators. These animals are distinguished by their many (eight or ten) tentacles or arms.

The mollusc family is well represented locally, and occupies a wide range of habitats. Common gastropods include the conch (*Strombus costatus*), the flame helmet (*Cassis flammea*), and the measled cowrie (*Cyprae zebra*). The latter is very attractive, and is the largest of the cowrie shells found in Bermuda. The flamingo tongue (*Cyphoma gibbosum*) is also a particular delight, often found on gorgonian fan corals. Nudibranchs, or sea-slugs, are a rare pleasure when sighted. They feed on a number of different animals and algae and are invariably brightly colored. One of the more common species is the sea goddess *(Hypselodoris bayeri)*. Octopus and squid are often observed in the open reefs at night. The squid particularly seems fascinated by divers' lights, or more likely, the food that these lights attract.

The flamingo tongue is one of the more common molluscs found feeding on sea fans.

The **Echinodermata**, or spiny-skinned animals, include sea stars *(Asteroidea)*, brittlestars *(Ophiuroidea)*, sea urchins *(Echinoidea)*, sea cucumbers *(Holothuroidea)*, and feather stars and sea lilies *(Crinoidea)*. These creatures move slowly on peculiar tube "feet" through a hydraulic-like network of water supplied by canals throughout the body. Crinoids, or feather stars, crawl out onto the coral surface as night falls. Brittle stars are sometimes found curled around the sea fans and sea whips. Basket stars extend their multi-jointed arms into the current to capture plankton, while sea urchins vie for space amidst the sponges and corals. Sea urchins often have other animals living among their spines, and are fascinating to observe (with care!).

The common sea star is found in the shallows around Flatts Bridge.

Chordates The phylum **Chordata** includes vertebrates and some of their more primitive relatives, such as the **Tunicata**—smooth, translucent, tube-shaped creatures that look like invertebrates, but are actually more closely allied with vertebrate animals like ourselves. This group includes the sea squirts and ascidians, some of the smallest of which are lightbulb tunicates (*Calavelina spp.*), which come in many different colors.

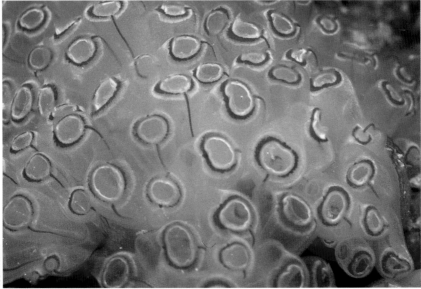

The purple sea squirt is a familiar sight in Bermudian waters.

Vertebrate Animals Two major groups of vertebrate animals are native to these waters–fishes and marine mammals. The latter are air breathers, and include whales, dolphins and porpoises, creatures that usually live on or near the surface, but are capable of diving to considerable depth. **Fishes** are divided into two principal groups. The cartilaginous fishes (*Chondrichthyes*; mainly sharks and rays) possess skeletons with no true bone (only cartilage) and have exposed, multiple gill openings. In contrast, the bony fishes (*Osteichthyes*) have skeletons consisting of a mixture of bone and cartilage, and have a single gill opening on each side of the body, covered by a hard, bony plate (*operculum*).

The following are brief descriptions of several of the more interesting or colorful **reef fishes**. Please note that a number of species are indeed poisonous or may sting or bite. Wild animals (and fish are no exception) should be observed cautiously. Many types of marine animals that do not move when you approach have means of defense such as sharp spines and stinging cells, so be careful and *never* touch!

Southern stingrays are most commonly found on the sand flats foraging for molluscs.

The most common **ray** found in the shallow waters of Bermuda is the southern stingray (*Dasyatis americana*). Stingrays are best observed after their regular "feeding frenzies" when they soon revert to their normal foraging behavior. There are three other, less common species of ray found here: the manta ray, eagle ray, and torpedo ray. **Sharks** are not commonly seen, but most frequently sighted is the nurse shark (*Ginglymostoma cirratum*), distinguishable by the two barbels on the top of its lip and small mouth. **Moray eels** are not particularly common around Bermuda, but there are a few. These creatures hide during the day and are active predators by night.

LAWSON WOOD

Goldentail moray eels are very shy and usually only come out at night to hunt.

They are easily approached and have the habit of opening and closing their mouth, which looks threatening, but is actually the way that they breathe. The spotted moray (*Gymnothorax moringa*) is perhaps the more commonly seen; the green moray (*Gymnothorax funebris*) is the largest. The goldentail moray (*Gymnothorax miliaris*) has small yellow spots over brown, its head often protrudes from the reef and it is the smallest of the Bermuda morays. The much rarer chain moray (*Echidna catenata*) is slightly larger with a large dark brown to black body with irregular yellow bars and yellow eyes. Snake eels live under the sand during the day and have a fin that runs along the length of their back. The goldspotted eel (*Myrichthys oculatus*) is another variety found here.

The **grouper** family is represented by some 13 species here; one of the most common varieties is the coney (*Cephalopholis fulvus*). This amusing

LAWSON WOOD

The coney goes through several color phases and is shown here in its rare golden phase.

LAWSON WOOD

Schoolmaster snapper stick together in schools around Bermuda's reefs and wrecks.

fish, which can grow up to 40 cm, appears to be always standing guard on a coral head waiting for a tasty morsel to swim by. Coneys come in many color variations, including dark reddish-brown and bright yellow.

Snapper, such as the schoolmaster (*Lutjanus apodus*) are often seen around wrecks in Bermudian waters, often in association with the bluestriped grunt (*Haemulon sciurus*). Perhaps the most common of the snapper family is the yellowtail snapper *(Ocyurus chrysurus)*. These inquisitive fish congregate in fairly large schools and often follow divers, looking for food and getting in the way of underwater photographers!

Yellowtail snapper are often found on the outer reefs.

Both **parrotfishes** (*Scaridae*) and **wrasses** *(Labridae)* are capable of sex reversal, changing from functional females to males. Such changes are generally accompanied by pronounced size and color changes, with males being the larger and more brightly colored. Parrotfish and wrasses come in a wide variety of sizes and colors. One of the larger species seen regularly is the stoplight parrotfish (*Sparisoma viride*), which may exceed 50 cm in length. In contrast, the princess parrotfish (*Scarus taeniopterus*) is quite small, growing only to about 32 cm. The largest member of the wrasse family in these waters is the hogfish (*Lachnolaimus maximus*). Large male hogfish can grow up to 1 meter in length and develop a pronounced snout and three long spines in the dorsal fin. Hogfish are often found accompanied by bar jacks. Other large species include the Spanish hogfish (*Bodianus rufus*), and the puddingwife (*Halichoeres radiatus*), which has greenish blue scrolls on its head and is blue-to-green overall, with a white mid-body bar occasionally present. It can grown up to 50 cm. There are many smaller species, such as the bluehead wrasse (*Thalassoma bifasciatum*). The young of this species are often seen in small social groups flitting among the coral heads.

Perhaps the fish we associate most with tropical coral reefs are **butterflyfishes** and **angelfishes**. With their disc-like

The puddingwife, one of the larger species of wrasse, often follows divers around the reef.

Colorful blue angelfish are common inside Flatts Bridge inlet.

Foureye butterflyfish, the smallest of the butterflyfish, are often flitting about reef tops.

bodies and brilliant colors, they definitely stand out. The rock beauty *(Holacanthus tricolor)* is a real beauty with its yellow face and tail and wide black body. It grows up to 30 cm and is fairly shy. The queen angelfish (*Holacanthus ciliariaris)* grows up to 45 cm and is particularly striking in color with an electric blue body running to gold fins, tail and face. It has a distinctive "crown" on its forehead. Queen angelfish are slow, moving among the sea fans and plumes. More commonly seen is the blue angelfish (*Holacanthus bermudensis*), which is without the distinctive crown. Five butterflyfishes are found in Bermudian waters. Two of the prettiest are the spotfin butterflyfish (*Chaetodon ocellatus*) and the four-eye butterflyfish (*Chaetodon capistratus*). The spotfin has a white body with a yellow trim and a black vertical band through the face and eye. The foureye has a large "eye" near the tail and is marked with numerous dark thin lines and a darker bar through the eye.

Among the most ubiquitous of reef fishes are the small **damselfishes**, many of which are highly territorial. The sergeant major (*Abudefduf saxatilis*), a small fish with five vertical black body bars is often very aggressive when protecting its eggs. This species always seems to appear when food is introduced. The yellowtail damselfish (*Microspathodon chrysurus*), a small, oval-shaped fish with a dark body and iridescent blue spots along the back and a yellow tail, is another protective parent.

Squirrelfish and soldierfish are fairly common around the reef and several of the species will congregate together in small numbers in caves and recesses. The common squirrelfish (*Holocentrus adscensionis*) has white triangular markings on the tips of its dorsal spines and is reddish in color, with light silvery stripes running horizontally along its body. The smooth trunkfish (*Lactophrys triqueter*) is another common reef dweller.

Silversides are small, schooling fishes often found in large numbers among the gullies and caves of the

Smooth trunkfish have few natural enemies.

reef. These are frequent prey for larger reef predators. Several species of **jacks**, including the bar jack (*Caranx ruber*), are often seen darting into schools of silversides, picking off fish at random and apparently working together in a pack. Bar jacks are fairly common in the coral heads. They are often in mating pairs, with one a silvery blue, the other almost completely black, looking and acting

A blanket of silversides is a great delight for any diver to encounter.

like the other's shadow. They often associate with the southern stingray and hogfish. Like many of the jacks, the Bermuda chub (*Kyphosus sectatrix*) is most often seen in fairly large schools cruising above the reef.

Among the largest of reef predators here is the great **barracuda** (*Sphyraena barracuda*). This aggressive-looking fish, with its long jaw and razor-sharp teeth, is usually solitary here, and can be found close to the mooring buoys where it will lie in wait under the shadow of a tied-up boat. Barracuda can grow up to 1.8 meters.

LAWSON WOOD

Barracuda are often found swimming around silversides.

Bermuda is also well known for its schools of **tarpon** (*Megalops atlanticus*), and several dive sites have been named after this aggressive hunter. Tarpon can grow to a maximum of 2.4 meters, although they are usually around 1 meter. Another predator, the **trumpetfish** (*Aulostomus maculatus*) is fairly common around the outer reefs. The trumpetfish grows up to 1.8 meters and has a number of color variations, ranging from yellow to an almost tartan pattern. It is distinguished by its long, trumpet-shaped mouth.

Hazardous Marine Life

LAWSON WOOD

Stinging Creatures Anemones, corals and jellyfish are armed with a battery of stinging cells (nematocists). These cells are actually tiny barbed harpoons tipped with a paralyzing poison, which the creature will fire into its prey should it happen to brush against it. These microscopic cells are particularly painful in the case of the Portuguese man-of-war (*Physalia physalis*), whose tentacles can trail underneath over 10 meters (30 ft). Its sting is very painful, similar to a bad bee sting except that you're likely to get stung more than once from the clusters of long tentacles. Even touching a Portuguese man-of-war a few hours after it's washed up on shore can result in burning stings. If you are stung, quickly remove the tentacles and apply vinegar or a meat tenderizer containing papain. For serious reactions, including chest pains or difficulty breathing, seek immediate medical attention.

LAWSON WOOD

Anemones are armed with stinging cells used to stun their prey.

Fire coral, often found growing over seafans, is easy to distinguish by its yellow finger-like columns and white tips covered with stinging hairs.

For many divers, the introduction to fire coral *(Millepora alcicornis)* can be a painful experience. Fire coral is not actually a true coral but a member of the hydroid family. It has a hard calcareous skeleton either branching or in bony plates. The "coral" is covered in thousands of tiny barbed hooks that can easily penetrate the skin and leave large irritations that last for several days. Learn to recognize and avoid this hazard.

A member of the anemone family is the warty corallimorph *(Discosoma sanctithomae)*, which is found under overhangs in a number of the shallower, frequently visited reefs and should be avoided. Likewise the attractive fire worm *(Hermodice carunculata)*, which has tiny piercing hairs in tufts all over the body, and can easily break off on the unwary diver's skin.

Warty corallimorphs look like small, flat anemones, but have powerful stinging cells.

Bearded fire worms have tufts of white hairs that can easily penetrate the skin.

LAWSON WOOD

The purple sea urchin usually occurs in shallow water.

Sea Urchins Wounds from sea urchin spines are unfortunately common for divers, particularly when diving in swell or surge that unavoidably push them into long-spined sea urchins *(Diadema antillarum)*. The spines are very sharp, and can penetrate wetsuits and booties. Once they've pierced the skin, they can snap off easily, so take care when removing the spines. The punctures are very painful, but usually not dangerous unless they become infected or penetrate deeply.

LAWSON WOOD

Nurse sharks are the most common sharks found in Bermuda.

Sharks Sharks are uncommonly seen in Bermuda, but are spotted on deeper dives near the edge of the continental shelf and the southern offshore seamounts. The most common shark is the relatively docile nurse shark *(Ginglymostoma cirratum)*, often seen sleeping in coral caves during the day. Argos Banks, to the south of

Bermuda, is one of the few locations where deepwater sharks are regularly found, such as the blue shark *(Prionace glauca)*, the shortfin mako *(Isurus oxyrinchus)* and the Galapagos shark *(Carcharhinus galapagensis)*.

Rays Stingrays are fairly uncommon, but are found in the shallow sand flats and eelgrass beds to the west of the island archipelago. They can inflict a nasty wound with their tail, but are usually very timid, and will not attack divers willingly. Never touch or grab the tail! Watch where you put your hands and feet and you should not have any problems with them.

Southern stingrays are armed with a stinger in their tail, but are considered harmless unless they are harrassed or stepped on.

LAWSON WOOD

An encounter with the large green moray eel is quite rare around Bermuda's reefs.

Eels Moray eels appear aggressive and threatening, due to their breathing pattern (opening and closing their mouths), yet they are rather gentle creatures with poor eyesight, venturing out from their holes only at night to feed. Eels are not dangerous unless you put your hand down carelessly on the coral in front of them, or try to handle or feed them. Eels have sharp teeth and strong jaws and may clamp down if someone thrusts a hand at them.

Scorpionfish Scorpionfish usually sit quietly among rocks and coral, looking more like rocks than fish. Though difficult to spot during the day, they can be seen more easily at night when divers' torches pick up the brightly colored pectoral fins. Scorpionfish have poisonous spines among their fins, so always watch where you put your hands. The sting is very painful, and can quickly infect, so seek medical attention as soon as possible if stung.

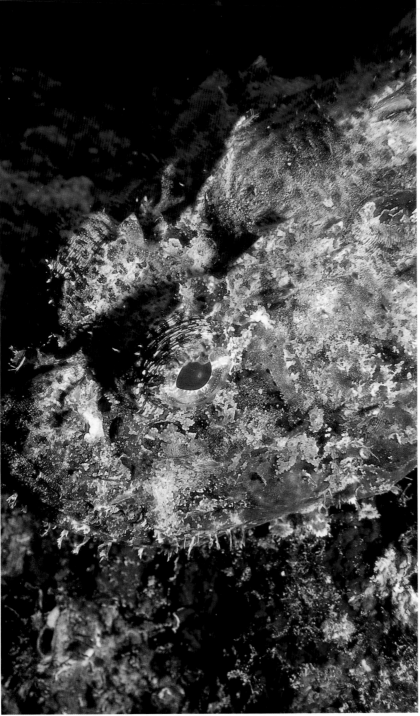

LAWSON WOOD

A master at camouflage, the scorpionfish is a common shallow water inhabitant.

Diving Conservation & Awareness

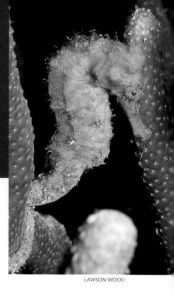

Marine Reserves

Moves to protect Bermuda's fragile reef systems began in 1960 to fight proposals to reclaim land on shallow reefs to the west and north of the island.

The Coral Reef Preserves Act of 1966 now protects all attached animals and plants found within the preservation areas. The largest shore site is the South Shore Coral Reef Preserve, which stretches from Hungry Bay to Gurnet Rock. The North Shore Coral Reef Preserve extends between Shelly Bay west to Commissioners Point and north to the outer reef edge, encompassing all of the area north to the North Rock Beacon. Another three seasonally protected areas exist at the southwestern area, the eastern area, and the northeastern area. All have important fisheries.

A number of specific dive sites have also been declared protected areas, and fishing boats are not allowed within a 500-1,000-meter radius. These are: South West Breaker; North Rock Beacon; and Eastern Blue Cut. The following shipwrecks are protected: the *Hermes*, the *Minnie Breslauer*, the *Kate*, the *Pelanion*, the *Zovetto*, the *Vixen* and the *Constellation*. The Walsinham Marine Reserve protects the mangroves and fringing reefs under the National Parks Act.

Large open caverns, like this one at Western Blue Cut are common on Bermuda's reefs.

Reef Etiquette

Dive sites tend to be located where the reefs and walls display the most beautiful corals and sponges. It only takes a moment—an inadvertently placed hand or knee on the coral or an unaware brush or kick with a fin—to destroy this fragile, living part of our delicate ecosystem. Please consider the following tips when diving and help preserve the ecology and beauty of the reefs:

1. Maintain proper buoyancy control and avoid over-weighting. Be aware that buoyancy can change over the period of an extended trip: initially you may breathe harder and need more weighting; a few days later you may breath more easily and need less weight.

2. Use correct weight belt position to stay horizontal, i.e., raise the belt above your waist to elevate your feet/fins, and move it lower toward your hips to lower them.

3. Use your tank position in the backpack as a balance weight, i.e., raise your backpack on the tank to lower your legs, and lower the backpack on the tank to raise your legs.

4. Be careful about buoyancy loss at depth; the deeper you go the more your wetsuit compresses, and the more buoyancy you lose.

Marine Conservation Organizations

Coral reefs and oceans are facing unprecedented environmental pressures. The following groups are actively involved in promoting responsible diving practices, publicizing environmental marine threats, and lobbying for better policies.

Project AWARE Foundation
☎ 714-540-0251
Website: www.projectaware.org

Cousteau Society
☎ 757-523-9335
Website: www.cousteau.org

CORAL: The Coral Reef Alliance
☎ 510-848-0110
Website: www.coral.org/

Ocean Futures
☎ 714-456-0790
Website: www.oceanfutures.org

Coral Forest
☎ 415-788-REEF
Website: www.blacktop.com/
 coralforest/

ReefKeeper International
☎ 305-358-4600
Website: www.reefkeeper.org

LAWSON WOOD

Although they look strong, sea fans can easily be damaged by a misplaced fin.

5. Photographers must be extra careful. Cameras and equipment affect buoyancy. Changing f-stops, framing a subject, and maintaining position for a photo often conspire to prohibit the ideal "no-touch" approach on a reef. So, when you must use "holdfasts," choose them intelligently (i.e., use one finger only for leverage off an area of dead coral).

6. Avoid full leg kicks when working close to the bottom and when leaving a photo scene. When you inadvertently kick something, stop kicking! Seems obvious, but some divers either semi-panic or are totally oblivious when they bump something. When treading water in shallow reef areas, take care not to kick up clouds of sand. Settling sand can easily smother the delicate organisms of the reef.

7. When swimming in strong currents, be extra careful about leg kicks and handholds.

8. Attach dangling gauges, computer consoles, and octopus regulators. They are like miniature wrecking balls to a reef.

9. Never drop boat anchors onto a coral reef, and take care not to ground boats on coral. Encourage dive operators and regulatory bodies to establish permanent moorings at popular dive sites.

10. Resist the temptation to collect or buy corals or shells. Aside from the ecological damage, taking home marine souvenirs depletes the beauty of a site and spoils the enjoyment of others.

11. Resist the temptation to feed fish. You may disturb their normal eating habits, encourage aggressive behavior, or feed them food that is detrimental to their health.

Although fish like this tiger grouper will readily eat out
of your hand, resist the temptation to feed them.

Underwater Photography & Video

LAWSON WOOD

Underwater Photography

Bermuda, with its year round clear water, super-abundance of wrecks, and excellent reef system, provides no shortage of subject matter for under-water photographers wishing to record their dives more accurately, or share their experiences with others.

Perhaps the best way to start is with a disposable camera, which is inex-pensive and will allow you to see your results quickly. These cameras work in shallow waters no deeper than about 2-10 meters (6-30 ft). Read the instructions carefully. Another option is to rent a waterproof housing, which will allow you to use the camera at depths to 30 meters (100 ft).

Submersible waterproof housings are always an option for your land camera. These can be bulky, but are strong, reliable and cheaper than a new underwater camera. You'll also need some sort of waterproof flash.

Whichever camera system you choose should be compatible and adapt-able with as much equipment as possible. You should consider not only the camera itself, but the lenses, flashes, and connecting parts. Before purchas-ing an expensive system, consider renting the equipment first to try it out.

Camera Care

When loading film into your camera, beware of cool, air-conditioned apart-ments. When you take the camera outside, the increase in temperature will cause the inside to condensate, i.e., "sweat." Simi-larly, don't leave your camera out in the sun, because when you take it under-water, the cool water temperature will also cause condensation on the inside of the lens or the housing's port.

Bermuda's largest dive shops have photo equipment for hire, and specialized classes in underwater photography and techniques are also offered. Whether you have an amphibi-ous-type system, such as the Nikonos or Sea & Sea system, or a housed land SLR camera, be sure to follow the proper pre-cautions: check that all of the connections are clean and that

The Beginner's Guide to Taking Underwater Photos

1. Consider your photography goals and buy the best system suitable for your anticipated needs.
2. Concentrate on mastering one technique at a time. Don't try to learn everything at once.
3. Record the technical details of your photos as you take them (an underwater slate is good for this) to see which settings get the best results.
4. When using fixed focus, pre-aim your flash out of the water whenever possible.
5. To avoid back-scatter in wide-angle photography, position the flash away from the camera body and at a 45° angle between the camera and subject. Never use the flash when the camera-to-subject distance is greater than one-fifth the underwater visibility.
6. Get as close as you can to your subject. Close-ups have the most impact and better color saturation.
7. To avoid shadows in close-up photography, bring the flash close to the subject and directly over the camera.
8. Never shoot downward. Always shoot horizontally or aim upward toward your subject.
9. Note the position of the sun when you enter the water. Use the sun to create back-lit shots to add depth and interest.
10. Be ruthless. The only way to really improve is by self criticism; put as much film through the camera as possible and learn from your mistakes.
11. Attend an underwater photography course.

all o-rings are free of dust, and apply a light coat of silicone grease. Also check for any nicks or cuts in the seals. Ensure that the flash fires correctly and that it has sufficient power to operate. When working with rechargeable flashes, make sure the recharger is compatible with the local electrical supply.

Generally, slide film is used for higher-quality photos, with film speeds of 50-100 ISO. This allows for better sharpness and color reproduction. For more casual shots, with less expensive equipment, print film is more often used, with film speeds of 200-400 ISO.

When taking underwater photos, control your buoyancy carefully, as a misplaced fin can knock against the coral and easily damage it.

Underwater Video

Virtually all of today's video systems are designed for on-land usage. The sophistication of underwater video lies in the waterproof housings developed for these systems. Housings come in a variety of styles and sizes. All have waterproof controls to allow you to use the camera's functions, but some are awkward to handle. If possible, buy a housing designed specifically for your camera. Since they are often heavy and cumbersome to carry, you should purchase a strong carrying case when you buy the housing.

With the introduction of digital Betacam video recording systems, image quality has greatly improved. It has also become much easier to edit videos, as the film can be run through a computer for virtually unlimited editing and special effects manipulation. (In fact, your only limitation may be your technical expertise.) You can even "snatch" single stills from your video film.

One advantage that video has over slide film is that there is no waste of film. You can reshoot your given subject time after time until you're pleased with the result. Remember, though, that video work quickly depletes the batteries. You should have at least two spare fully charged battery packs each time you enter the water.

Video lights have also improved a great deal. Lights are now small and lightweight, with a separate battery power pack that can be attached to your air tank or held underneath the housing for better stability.

Plan your shooting sequences before entering the water and follow that plan as best you can. Of course, there is always the chance that something totally unexpected will happen (or swim by!) and you should be ready for all possibilities. Avoid diving with inexperienced divers or trainees, as they will inevitably slow you down. Train your buddy to assist you.

Try not to prolong the sequence you are filming. An overly long sequence is boring and difficult to edit. Take small vignettes of marine life studies, which are much easier to edit than long sequences. Keep the movement direction of divers constant and whenever possible have the divers and fish swim *toward* the camera. Have your buddy/model swim toward you from the other side of the reef. As he/she approaches, the fish in front of the diver will also find themselves swimming toward you, making for a more interesting shot. When working close to small subjects, place the camera on a small tripod to avoid camera shake.

When editing your video, be ruthless with your choice of clips. Learn from wildlife films and study the way experts edit sequences. Use a professional sound track to enhance your film work and keep your video to under 30 minutes. Consider using someone else's voice to add a touch of professionalism.

LAWSON WOOD

Bermuda's reefs are littered with cannons and debris from a long history of shipwrecks.

Listings

Accommodations

The following is a representative, not exhaustive, list of accommodations, all of which are located in the vicinity of the dive shops and have good amenities,

including restaurants. The full list of hotels, guest houses, cottages, self-catering apartments and even private islands for hire can be obtained from any of the Bermuda Tourist offices. The islands' dive centers are also part of the Bermuda Central Reservation Services that can be contacted directly at ☎ 800-637-4116; Fax: 441-236-1662; Email: reservations@bspl.bm.

Large Hotels

Elbow Beach Bermuda
P.O. Box HM 455, Hamilton HM BX
☎ 441-236-3535 Fax: 441-236-8043

Grotto Bay Beach Hotel and Tennis Club
11 Blue Hole Hill, Hamilton CR 04
☎ 441-293-8333 Fax: 441-293-2306

Hamilton Princess Hotel
P.O. Box HM 837, Hamilton HM CX
☎ 441-295-3000 Fax: 441-295-1914

Marriott's Castle Harbour Resort
P.O. Box HM 841, Hamilton HM CX
☎ 441-293-2040 Fax: 441-293-8288

Sonesta Beach Resort
P.O. Box HM 1070, Hamilton HM EX
☎ 441-238-8122 Fax: 441-238-8463

Southampton Princess
P.O. Box HM 1379, Hamilton HM FX
☎ 441-238-8000 Fax: 441-238-8968

Small Hotels

Palm Reef Hotel
P.O. Box HM 1189, Hamilton HM EX
☎ 441-236-1000 Fax: 441-236-6392

Palmetto Hotel & Cottages
P.O. Box FL 54, Smith's FL BX
☎ 441-293-2323 Fax: 441-293-8761

Rosedon
P.O. Box HM 290, Hamilton HM AX
☎ 441-295-1640 Fax: 441-295-5940

Royal Palms Hotel
P.O. Box HM 499, Hamilton HM CX
☎ 441-292-1854 Fax: 441-292-1946

The Reefs
56 South Rd., Southampton SN 02
☎ 441-238-0222 Fax: 441-238-8372

Willowbank
P.O. Box MA 296, Sandys MA BX
☎ 441-234-1616 Fax: 441-234-3373

Cottages

Cambridge Beaches
30 King's Point Rd., Somerset MA 02
☎ 441-234-0331 Fax: 441-234-3352

Lantana
P.O. Box SB 90, Somerset Bridge SB BX
☎ 441-234-0141 Fax: 441-234-2562

Marley Beach Cottages
South Shore Rd., P.O. Box PG 278,
Paget PG BX
☎ 441-236-1143 Fax: 441-236-1984

Self-catering Apartments

Greenbank
Salt Kettle Rd., P.O. Box PG 201,
Paget PG BX
☎ 441-236-3615 Fax: 441-236-2427

Longtail Cliffs
South Shore Rd., P.O. Box HM 836,
Hamilton HM CX
☎ 441-236-2822 Fax: 441-236-5178

Dining

The most popular restaurants also tend to be situated in the major international hotels (many of which are listed above). The following are lower-priced eateries, where the food is good and you don't need to get dressed up.

M. R. Onions
Par-La-Ville Rd.
Hamilton
☎ 441-292-5021
(ribs and seafood)

The Ice Queen
Rural Hill Plaza
Paget
☎ 441-236-3136
(sandwiches and BBQ)

The Harbourfront
Front St. West
Hamilton
☎ 441-295-4207
(surf & turf)

Kathy's
69 Front St.
Hamilton
☎ 441-295-5203
(fish, pasta)

Dinty's lunch wagons
found at many beaches,
parks, etc.
(burgers, fries)

New Queen
Par-La-Ville Rd.
Hamilton
☎ 441-295-4004
(Chinese)

Pinks Deli
55 Front St.
Hamilton
☎ 441-295-3524
(salads, sandwiches)

Pizza Dudes
Hamilton/Paget stoplight
☎ 441-232-DUDE
(pizzas, subs, salads)

The Porch
93 Front St.
Hamilton
☎ 441-292-4737
(grills, surf & turf)

The Theatre
Cafe, 12 Queen St.
Hamilton
☎ 441-292-6497
(chicken, ribs, burgers)

The Spot
Burnaby St.
Hamilton
☎ 441-292-6293
(grills, sandwiches, salads)

Sunsets
Ocean View Golf Club
Barker's Hill
Devonshire
☎ 441-295-1911
(Bermudian cuisine)

La Trattoria
Washington Lane
Hamilton
☎ 441-295-1877
(Italian)

Swizzle Inn
stop before Causeway
Blue Hole Hill
☎ 441-293-9300
(grills, fries, rum swizzles)

Lighthouse Cafe
Gibbs Hill Lighthouse
☎ 441-238-8679

Diving Services

Blue Water Divers
P.O. Box SN165, Southampton SN BX
Location: Robinson's Marina next to Somerset Bridge in Sandys Parish
☎ 441-234-1034 Fax: 441-234-3561
Email: bwdivers@ibl.bm
Website: www.divebermuda.com
Certification: PADI, NAUI, SSI
Services: Retail and rental gear
Boats: One 42-ft boat, one 36-ft boat, one 33-ft boat
Affiliated hotels: Cambridge Beaches, The Reefs Hotel, Pompano Beach Club, Marriott's Castle Harbour Hotel, Elbow Beach Bermuda

Fantasea Diving & Snorkeling
1 Harbour Rd., Paget PG01
Location: Darrell's Wharf on the Warwick Ferry route
☎ 441-236-6339; 888-DO-A-DIVE (toll free); Fax: 441-236-8926
Email: fantasea@ibl.bm
Website: www.Bermuda-Watersports.com/fantasea
Certification: PADI 5-star facility, BSAC
Services: Retail and rental gear
Boats: One 40-ft boat
Affiliated hotels: Elbow Beach Bermuda, Palm Reef Hotel

Nautilus Diving Ltd.
P.O. Box HM 237, Hamilton HM AX
Location: retail store at the Hamilton Princess Hotel shopping arcade; dive centers at the Hamilton Princess Hotel dock and Southampton Princess beach
☎ 441-295-9485 Fax: 441-234-5180
Email: choskins@ibl.bm
Website: www.bermuda.bm
Certification: PADI 5-star facility, IDC
Services: Retail and rental gear
Boats: Two 40-ft boats
Affiliated hotels: the Hamilton Princess Hotel, Southampton Princess

Scuba Look
P.O. Box 685, Warwick WK BX
Location: Grotto Bay Beach Hotel dock
☎ 441-293-7319 Fax: 441-295-2421
Email: scubaluk@ibl.com
Website: www.diveguideint.com/p0078.htm
Certification: PADI training facility
Services: Retail and rental gear
Boats: One 45-ft boat
Affiliated hotel: Grotto Bay Beach Hotel

South Side Scuba Watersports
Sonesta Beach Resort, South Shore Rd., Southampton
Location: Sonesta Beach Resort beach front
☎ 441-238-1833 Fax: 441-236-0394
Email: southsid@ibl.com
Website: www.Bermuda-Watersports.com
Certification: NAUI dive center and PADI training facility
Services: Retail and rental gear
Boats: One 35-ft boat
Affiliated hotel: Sonesta Beach Resort

Club
British Sub-Aqua Club
P.O. Box 521, Devonshire DV BX
(Admiralty House Park)
☎ 441-293-9531
The club has weekly instructional meetings, frequent dives, and offers visiting
BSAC members the use of its facilities

Tourist Offices

The Bermuda Department of Tourism, in cooperation with the Chamber
of Commerce, operates the following tourist offices:

Bermuda Department of Tourism (Head Office)
Global House, 43 Church St., Hamilton HM12
☎ 441-292-0023 Fax: 441-292-7537

Hamilton Visitors Service Bureau
Front St., Hamilton
☎ 441-295-1480

St. George's Visitors Service Bureau
King's Square, St. George
☎ 441-297-1642

Dockyards Visitors Service Bureau
No.10 Dockyard Terrace
☎ 441-234-3824

Visitors Service Bureau
Bermuda International Airport, St. George
☎ 441-293-0736

The Bermuda Department of Tourism operates the following offices abroad:

Canada
1200 Bay St., Suite 1004, Toronto, Ontario M5R 2A5
☎ 416-923-9600 Fax: 416-923-4840

Germany
Herzogspitalstrasse 5, 80331 München
☎ 89-23-66-21-32 Fax: 89-26-04-009

Sweden
Drottninggatan 31, 2-411 14
☎ 46-31-13-18-10 Fax: 46-31-711-04-56

United Kingdom
1 Battersea Church Rd., London SW11 3LY
☎ 44-0171-771-7001 Fax: 44-0171-771 7037

U.S.A.
Head Office:
310 Madison Ave., Suite 201, New York, NY 10017
☎ 212-818-9800; 800-223-6106 Fax: 212-983-5289

Regional offices:
245 Peachtree Center, Avenue NE, Suite 803, Atlanta, GA 30303
☎ 404-524-1541 Fax: 404-524-1541

44 School St., Suite 1010, Boston, MA 02108
☎ 617-742-0405 Fax: 617-723-7786

150 N. Wacker Drive, Suite 1070, Chicago, IL 60606
☎ 312-782-5486 Fax: 312-704-6996

3151 Cahuenga Blvd West, Suite 111, Los Angeles, CA 90068
☎ 213-436-0744 / 800-252-0211 (from CA); 800-421-0000
(from elsewhere in the U.S.) Fax: 213-436-0750

Publications

Natural History

Marine Flora and Fauna of Bermuda, Wolfgang Sterrer,
John Wiley & Sons, 1986

Bermuda's Marine Life, Bermuda Zoological Society, 1992

Reef Creature Identification, Paul Humann, New World Publications, Inc.,1992

Reef Fish Identification, Paul Humann, New World Publications, Inc., 1994

Reef Coral Identification, Paul Humann, New World Publications, Inc., 1993

Pisces Guide to Watching Fishes, Roberta Wilson and James Q. Wilson, Gulf Publishing Co., 1992

Pisces Guide to Venomous & Toxic Marine Life of the World, Cunningham and Goetz, Gulf Publishing Co., 1996

Wonders of the Deep (Underwater Bermuda), Burke *et al*, Boulton Publishing Services, 1988

Bermuda History

Bermuda's Story, Terry Tucker, 1959

Bermuda Shipwrecks, Daniel and Denise Berg, Aqua Explorers, Inc., 1991

The Wreck of the Sea Venture, William Zuill, Global Press Ltd., 1972

Shipwreck, Ivor Noel Hume, Capstan Pub., 1995

Shipwrecks of the Western Hemisphere, Robert F. Marx, World Publishing Co., 1971

Bermuda, Scott Stallard, Boulton Publishing Services, 1989

Travel

Aqua Expeditions, Wendy Canning Church, Divers Exchange Int., 1994

Bermuda, Bendure and Friary, Lonely Planet Publications, 1997

Diving Bermuda, Cancelmo and Strohofer, Aqua Quest, 1990

Periodicals

Bermudian Magazine (glossy monthly)

Neptune's Notes, Bermuda Sub Aqua Club (bi-monthly)

North Rock Magazine, Bermudian Publishing Co. (quarterly)

Preview Bermuda (monthly)

Quarterly, Bermuda Maritime Museum

This Week in Bermuda (weekly guide)

Vacation Bermuda hotel edition

Shipwreck Registry

LAWSON WOOD

The following is a list of the 160 best documented shipwrecks of Bermuda, and their country of origin:

Name of Ship	Date Lost	Country of Origin
La Bermuda	1500-1510 (est.)	Spain
Unknown Spanish nao	1533	Spain
Unknown	1543	Portugal
Unknown Spanish nao	1550	Spain
Santa Barbola	1551	Spain
Capitana	1560	Spain
Unknown Spanish nao	1563	Spain
Unknown Portuguese	1580	Portugal
Santa Lucia	1584	Spain
Unknown Spanish nao	1588	Spain
Unknown French	1593	France
San Pedro	1596	Spain
Unidentified	1603	Spain
Santa Ana	1605	Spain
Sea Venture	1609	England
Unknown	1619	Netherlands
Warwick	1619	England
San Antonio	1621	England
San Ignacio	1622	Spain
N.S. de la Limpia Conception	1622	Spain
Seaflower	1623	England
La Viga	1639	Spain
pattachuelo El Galgo	1639	Spain
Unknown	1644	Spain
Eagle	1659	England
Virginia Mercheant	1660	England
Unknown Spanish nao	1669	Spain
San Salvador	1684	Spain
Friendship	1744	England
Mary and Hannah	1744	England
Tryton	1747	England

Dorothy and Elizabeth	1747	England/America
Leoftoffe	1749	England
Margaret	1750	England
Manilla	1753	Denmark
Mary	1757	England
Hunter's Galley	1757	America
Brittania	1758	England
Manchineel	1760	France
Griffin	1761	England
Judith Maria	1762	England
Katherine	1763	England
Peggy	1764	England
Duke	1765	Unknown (sailing to Portugal)
Fairfax	1766	England
Elizabeth	1766	England
Penn	1768	America
Martin + one other	1769	England
Allitude	1769	America
Industry	1774	England
Repulse	1777	England
Mark Antonio	1777	Spain
Sir George Arthur	1778	England
Lord Amherst	1778	England
Nancy	1779	England
50 wrecked ships during hurricane	1780	Unknown
Unknown	1780	France
Lord Frederick	1781	England
H.M.S. Cereberus	1783	England
H.M.S. Pallas	1783	England
H.M.S. Mentor	1783	England
Stadt Cortrycht	1783	England
Betsey	1784	Scotland
Lord Donegal	1784	Ireland
Kingston	1786	U.S.A.
Swift	1787	Unknown (sailing from Grenada)
Unknown large number of ships during hurricane	1788	Unknown, possibly England
Marie Therese	1790	France
Le Grand Aanictl	1792	France
Actif	1794	England
George Douglas	1794	Unknown (sailing from Havana)
Harriet	1794	Unknown
Minerva + two others	1795	U.S.A./England
Polly	1796	U.S.A.
Nancy	1796	U.S.A.
Humber	1800	U.S.A.

Dispatch	1801	U.S.A.
Ebenezer	1801	Unknown (sailing to Santo Domingo)
Mary Ann	1801	Unknown (sailing from U.S.A.)
Commerce	1802	U.S.A.
Roebuck	1802	U.S.A.
Margaret	1803	U.S.A.
Providence	1804	England
Surprise	1804	Unknown
Hunter	1805	U.S.A.
Pamela	1806	France
Loyal Sam	1806	England
Three Friends	1806	U.S.A.
H.M.S. Subtle	1807	England
Rosannah	1807	U.S.A.
Merchant	1807	Unknown (sailing from U.S.A.)
Batavia	1808	Unknown (sailing to England)
William Grey	1809	England
William & Mary	1810	England
Montgomery	1811	Unknown (sailing from England)
Frederick	1811	Unknown (sailing from New York)
Eliza	1811	Unknown (sailing from New York)
H.M.S. Barbados	1812	England
Pensacola del Sol	1812	Spain
Antonia	1812	Spain
Lady Emily	1813	England
Pacific	1813	England
H.M.S. Dominica	1815	England
Duke of Wellington	1816	England
Peter	1817	Unknown
Elizabeth	1817	Unknown (sailing to U.S.A.)
Emma	1817	Unknown (sailing from New York)
Caesar	1818	England
Hope	1818	U.S.A.
Alfred the Great	1818	England
Admiral Durham	1818	England
Mary	1818	U.S.A.
Unknown	1818	England
Lydia	1819	France
St. Helena	1819	Unknown (sailing from Jamaica)

Hamilton	1819	England
Pallas	1821	U.S.A.
Indian Chief	1822	U.S.A.
Vriendscaap	1823	Netherlands
Collector	1823	U.S.A.
Mary	1823	U.S.A.
Cyno	1824	U.S.A.
L'Herminie	1839	France
Minerva	1849	Unknown (possibly England)
Curlew	1856	England
Nola	1863	Scotland/U.S.A.
Marie Celestia	1864	England/U.S.A.
Beaumaris Castle	1873	England
Minnie Breslauer	1873	England
Early Riser	1876	Unknown (possibly England)
Alert	1877	England
Kate	1878	England
Lartington	1879	England
North Carolina	1880	England
Darlington	1886	England
Richard P. Buck	1889	U.S.A.
Apollo	1890	Unknown (sailing to U.S.A.)
Vixen	1896	England
Madiana	1903	Scotland/Canada
Pollockshields	1916	Germany/England
Blanch King	1920	U.S.A.
Taunton	1920	Norway
Caraquet	1923	U.S.A.
Zovetto	1924	Italy
Mussel	1926	Bermuda
Cristóbol Colón	1936	Spain
Iristo	1937	Norway
Pelinaion	1939	Greece
Constellation	1942	U.S.A.
Col. William Ball	1943	Bermuda
Grotto Bay barges	1946	Bermuda
Wychwood	1955	U.S.A.
Elda	1956	U.S.A.
B-29 bomber	1961	U.S. air base on Bermuda
Ramona	1967	U.S.A.
Hermes	1984	U.S.A./Bermuda
King Bermuda	1984	U.S.A./Bermuda
Triton ferry	1988	Bermuda
Xing Da	1997	China

Index

dive sites covered in this book appear in **bold** type

A

accommodations 23, 112-113
Admirality Park 29
anemone 86, 98-99
   - giant 86
   - corkscrew 86
   - warty corallimorph 86, 99
angelfish 93-95
   - blue 62, 94, 95
   - rock beauty 95
   - queen 95
annelida (worms) 86
Arboretum, The 29
Argos Banks 41
arrow crab 54
arthropoda 87-88

B

B-29 Bomber 59
banks 25
barracuda 97
Beaches, North Shore 33
   - Tobacco Bay
   - Shelly Bay
   - Admirality House
Beaches, South Shore 32-33
   - Elbow
   - Horseshoe Bay
   - Warwick Long Bay
   - Jobson's Cove, Stonehole Bay
   - John Smith's Bay
   - Clearwater Beach
   - Astwood
   - Church Bay
   - West Whale Bay
   - Mangrove Bay
   - Maritime Museum Snorkel Trail
benthic 88
Bermuda Archives 37

Bermuda Biological Station for
   Research 31
Bermuda Central Reservation Services 112
Bermuda Historical Society Museum 37
Bermuda Library 37
Bermuda Maritime Museum 30
Bermuda Railway Trail 29
Bermuda shorts 26
Bermuda Underwater Exploration
   Institute 30,37
birdwatching 28
Blue Hole (*see **Eastern Blue Cut***)
bommies (*see patch reef*)
Botanical Gardens 28-29
breaker 40
British Sub-Aqua Club 41, 115
butterflyfish 93-95
   - foureye 94, 95
   - spotfin 95

C

Caesar 58
camera equipment (*see photography*)
Cathedral
cave diving 41
caves 31
   - Crystal Caves
   - Leamington's Amber Caves
cephalopods 88
chordates 89
Chub Heads 54
clothing 26-27
cnidaria 85
coelenterata (*see cnidaria*)
Constellation 48
coral 85-86, 98-99
   - brain 78
   - fire 99
   - star 86
crinoids 89

Cristóbol Colón 78-79

crustacean 87-88

D

damselfish 95

- yellowtail 95

- sergeant major 95

DAN (Diver's Alert Network) 39

Darlington 55

Devil's Hole 81

Devonshire (*see parishes*)

dining 114

dive ratings 43

dive shops, services 114-115

- Blue Water Divers 34, 114

- Fantasea Diving/Snorkeling 34, 114

- Nautilus Diving Ltd. 114

- Scuba Look 114

- South Side Scuba Watersports 115

Dockyards Snorkel Park 56

E

Eastern Blue Cut 48

echinodermata 89

eels 90-91, 102

- spotted moray 91

- green moray 91, 102

- goldentail moray 91

- chain moray 91

- snake eel 91

- goldspotted eel 91

electricity 26

Ely's Harbour 29

F

fish feeding 62, 107

fire coral (*see coral*)

fire worm (*see worms*)

flamingo tongue 88

flash use (*see photography*)

Flatt's Bridge 82

Flatts Bridge Aquarium,
    Museum & Zoo 31

flights 22-23

Fogo Brava (*see **Hermes***)

food 24

Fort St. Catherine 17

fringing reef 40

G

gastropoda 88

Ginger Beer Bottle (*see **Manilla***)

goby 86

golf 28

Grotto Bay Barges 80-81

grouper 91-93

- coneys 91-93

H

Hamilton (*see parishes*)

Hamilton, City of 12

Hangover Hole 70

hazardous marine life 98-103

helmet diving 30

hermit crab 87-88

hiking 28-29

history 14

Hole in the Wall 67

hospital 25-26

hotels (*see accommodation*s)

hyperbaric recompression facility
    (*see recompression chamber*)

I

Inbetweenies 62

invertebrate animals 84-89

J

jacks 95-96

jellyfish 85, 98-99

K

King 65

L

L'Herminie 53

Lartington 52

lobster 87-88

- spiny 87-88
- slipper 88

M

Madiana 79-80
Manilla (Ginger Beer Bottle) 77-78
marine conservation 104-107
    - organizations 105
marine reserves 104
    - South Shore Coral Reef 104
    - North Shore Coral Reef 104
    - Walsinham Marine 104
Mary Celestia 63-64
measurements 26
Minnie Breslauer 68-69
mollusca 88
money 24
Montana (*see Nola*)
moray eel (*see eel*)

N

Nassa Point 75
nematocists 85, 98
Nola (Montana) 50-51
North Carolina 60
nudibranch 88

P

parishes 12
Paget (*see parishes*)
parrotfish 93
    - blue 48
    - princess 93
    - stoplight 93
passport 19
patch reef 40
peacock flounder 69
Pelinaion 27-28
Pembroke (*see parishes*)
Penhurst Park 29
photography 27, 108-111
    - processing 27
    - video 109-110

pipefish 56
Pollockshields 73
Polychaetes 86
Porifera (sponges) 84
publications 116-117
pufferfish 74
purple sea squirt 89

R

ray 90, 101
    - manta 90
    - southern stingray 90, 101
    - eagle 90
    - torpedo 90
recompression chamber 26, 38-39
reef fishes 90
resort courses 36
restaurants (*see dining*)
Rita Zovetta (*see Zovetto*)
Royal Bermuda Yacht Club 29

S

safety 38
sailing 29
Sandy Hole 66
Sandys (*see parishes*)
sargassumfish 81
scorpionfish 102, 103
sea cucumbers 89
sea fans 86
sea goddess (*see nudibranch*)
sea slugs (*see nudibranch*)
sea stars 89
sea urchin 89, 100
Sea Venture 14-16
shark 90, 100
    - nurse 90, 100
    - blue 101
    - shortfin mako 101
    - Galapagos 101
Shell Hole 67
shipwreck registry 118-121
shrimp 87
    - anemone 42

- banded coral 87
- Pederson's cleaner 66
- Periclemines 87
- red hingeback 87
silversides 42, 95, 96
Smith's (*see parishes*)
Southhampton (*see parishes*)
snapper 93
- bluestriped grunt 93
- yellowtail 93
- schoolmaster 92, 93
snorkeling 48, 50, 52, 53, 56, 57, 66, 67,
  70, 73, 80, 81, 82
Somers, George 14
South West Breaker 60
Spittal Pond 28
sponges 84
spotted drum 70
squirrelfish 95
St. George 12, 23
St. George's (*see parishes*)
stingray (*see rays*)

T

tarpon 97
Taunton 77
The Deep 48, 50
time 25
tourist offices 115-116
transportation 22-23
trumpetfish 97

trunkfish 95
Tucker, Teddy 30, 53, 58
tunicata 89

V

vertebrate animals 90-95
video (*see photography*)
visibility 13
Vixen 57

W

Warwich (*see parishes*)
water temperature 19
weather 19
wetsuit 26
whale watching 31
worms 86
- bluehead 76, 93
- Christmas tree 86
- fire worm 99
wrasse 93
- bluehead 76, 93
- hogfish 93
- puddingwife 93

X

Xing Da 83

Z

Zovetto 76-77

Lonely Planet Pisces Books

The **Diving & Snorkeling Guides** are dive guides to top destinations worldwide. Beautifully illustrated with full-color photos throughout, the series explores the best diving and snorkeling areas and prepares divers for what to expect when they get there. Each site is described in detail, with information on suggested ability levels, depth, visibility, and, of course, marine life. There's basic topside information as well for each destination. Don't miss the guides to:

Australia: Coral Sea & Great Barrier Reef

Australia: Southeast Coast

Bahamas: Family Islands & Grand

Bahamas: Nassau & New Providence

Bali & the Komodo Region

Belize

Bermuda

Best Caribbean Diving

Bonaire

British Virgin Islands

Cayman Islands

Cocos Island

Cozumel

Cuba

Curaçao

Fiji

Florida Keys

Florida's East Coast

Guam & Yap

Hawaiian Islands

Jamaica

Northern California & Monterey Peninsula

Pacific Northwest

Palau

Puerto Rico

Red Sea

Roatan & Honduras' Bay Islands

Scotland

Seychelles

Southern California

St. Maarten, Saba, & St. Eustatius

Texas

Truk Lagoon

Turks & Caicos

U.S. Virgin Islands

Vanuatu

Plus illustrated natural history guides:

Pisces Guide to Caribbean Reef Ecology

Great Reefs of the World

Sharks of Tropical & Temperate Seas

Venomous & Toxic Marine Life of the World

Watching Fishes

Lonely Planet Series Descriptions

Lonely Planet **travel guides** explore a destination in depth with options to suit a range of budgets. With reliable, practical advice on getting around, restaurants and accommodations, these easy-to-use guides also include detailed maps, color photographs, extensive background material and coverage of sites both on and off the beaten track.

For budget travelers **shoestring guides** are the best single source of travel information covering an entire continent or large region. Written by experienced travelers these 'tried and true' classics offer reliable, first-hand advice on transportation, restaurants and accommodations, and insider tips for avoiding bureaucratic confusion and stretching money as far as possible.

City guides cover many of the world's great cities with full-color photographs throughout, front and back cover gatefold maps, and information for every traveler's budget and style. With information for business travelers, all the best places to eat and shop and itinerary suggestions for long and short-term visitors, city guides are a complete package.

Lonely Planet **phrasebooks** have essential words and phrases to help travelers communicate with the locals. With color tabs for quick reference, an extensive vocabulary, use of local scripts and easy-to-follow pronunciation instructions, these handy, pocket-sized language guides cover most situations a traveler is likely to encounter.

Lonely Planet **walking guides** cover some of the world's most exciting trails. With detailed route descriptions including degrees of difficulty and best times to go, reliable maps and extensive background information, these guides are an invaluable resource for both independent hikers and those in organized groups.

Lonely Planet **travel atlases** are thoroughly researched and fact-checked by the guidebook authors to ensure they complement the books. And the handy format means none of the holes, wrinkles, tears, or constant folding and refolding of flat maps. They include background information in five languages.

Journeys is a new series of travel literature that captures the spirit of a place, illuminates a culture, recounts an adventure and introduces a fascinating way of life. Written by a diverse group of writers, they are tales to read while on the road or at home in your favorite armchair.

Entertaining, independent and adventurous, Lonely Planet **videos** encourage the same approach to travel as the guidebooks. Currently broadcast throughout the world, this award-winning series features all original footage and music.

Where to Find Us . . .

Lonely Planet is known worldwide for publishing practical, reliable and no-nonsense travel information in our guides and on our web site. The Lonely Planet list covers just about every accessible part of the world. Currently there are nine series: *Pisces guides, travel guides, shoestring guides, walking guides, city guides, phrasebooks, audio packs, travel atlases* and *Journeys*–a unique collection of travel writing.

Lonely Planet Publications

Australia
PO Box 617, Hawthorn 3122, Victoria
☎ (03) 9819 1877 fax (03) 9819 6459
e-mail talk2us@lonelyplanet.com.au

USA
150 Linden Street
Oakland, California 94607
☎ (510) 893 8555, (800) 275 8555
fax (510) 893 8563
e-mail info@lonelyplanet.com

UK
10A Spring Place,
London NW5 3BH
☎ (0171) 428 4800 fax (0171) 428 4828
e-mail go@lonelyplanet.co.uk

France
71 bis rue du Cardinal Lemoine,
75005 Paris
☎ 01 44 32 06 20 fax 01 46 34 72 55
e-mail bip@lonelyplanet.fr

World Wide Web: www.lonelyplanet.com or **AOL keyword: lp**